Praise for

MEDIA CIRCUS

"Kim takes us to a place the camera rarely has an opportunity to go. An intimate look inside the lives of grieving survivors with a level of trust only a fellow survivor could earn. At times of tragedy, mass media tends to skim the surface. Kim goes deep into the most private thoughts of people who both want to be left alone, yet have a remarkable story to tell."
—**Kyra Phillips, CNN Anchor/Correspondent**

"Behind every headline lies a personal story that is often forgotten or never told. Kim Goldman's *Media Circus* renders an eye-opening glance into the reality of high-profile victims' personal loss and struggle for healing."
—**Debra Tate, victim advocate and author of *Sharon Tate: Recollection***

"*Media Circus* is a fantastic read about living through, surviving, and recovering from trauma. Goldman makes very important comparisons of cases from the past 30 years and shows how social media and media in general has impacted the victims while living under the public microscope."
—**Katie Beers, author and victims' rights advocate**

MEDIA
CIRCUS

MEDIA CIRCUS

A Look at Private Tragedy in the Public Eye

KIM GOLDMAN

with Tatsha Robertson

BenBella Books, Inc.
Dallas, TX

BenBella

BenBella Books, Inc.
10300 N. Central Expressway
Suite #530
Dallas, TX 75231
www.benbellabooks.com
Send feedback to feedback@benbellabooks.com

Printed in the United States of America
10 9 8 7 6 5 4 3 2 1

Library of Congress Cataloging-in-Publication Data:
Goldman, Kim.
  Media circus : a look at private tragedy in the public eye / Kim Goldman, with Tatsha Robertson.
     pages cm
  Includes bibliographical references and index.
  ISBN 978-1-941631-60-7 (hardback)—ISBN 978-1-942952-00-8 (electronic)
1. Victims of crimes in mass media. 2. Mass media and crime. 3. Bereavement.
4. Families—Press coverage. 5. Privacy, Right of. I. Title.
  HV6250.25.G645 2015
  070.4'4936288—dc23
                                2015016705

Editing by Leah Wilson
Copyediting by Shannon Kelly
Proofreading by Alda Trabucchi, Clarissa Phillips, and Brittney Martinez
Text design by Publishers' Design and Production Services, Inc.

Text composition by Integra Software Services Pvt. Ltd.
Cover design by Faceout Studio, Emily Weigel
Jacket design by Sarah Dombrowsky
Printed by Lake Book Manufacturing

Distributed by Perseus Distribution
www.perseusdistribution.com

To place orders through Perseus Distribution:
Tel: (800) 343-4499
Fax: (800) 351-5073
E-mail: orderentry@perseusbooks.com

Significant discounts for bulk sales are available. Please contact Glenn Yeffeth at glenn@benbellabooks.com or (214) 750-3628.

To the victims and survivors of violent crime,
your poise and bravery in the face of adversity
and trauma is admirable and inspiring.

CONTENTS

COLLENE CAMPBELL

SCOTT AND KATHLEEN LARIMER, SHIRLEY WYGAL

ESAW AND EMERALD GARNER

TERE DUPERRAULT FASSBENDER

INTRODUCTION

I want to share with you several stories, but not the stories you might expect from me.

Yes, I could share the one about my father, Fred Goldman, a salesman at the time, driving for hours in his white Mitsubishi 3000 up and down the Ventura Freeway in Southern California on June 13, 1994, listening to talk radio reports about Nicole Brown Simpson, the wife of famous ex-football player O. J. Simpson, found slaughtered alongside an unidentified male. "Another murder in Los Angeles," he thought sadly, as he pulled into his next appointment, unaware that in just a few short hours his son Ron's driver's license picture would be plastered on every channel, revealing him as that "unidentified male."

I could tell you how I saw images of the Brentwood crime scene on television that same day as I ate my lunch in the Wells Fargo break room in San Francisco, not realizing it was my brother's mutilated body beneath the bloody sheet.

I could talk about the mob of reporters that regularly settled in for the day in their satellite trucks outside our home in the quiet Los Angeles suburb of Agoura. With their microphones and cameras, journalists from every news outlet were just waiting for something to write about us. Just waiting. The questions never stopped: "Did you know O. J. Simpson?" "What was Ron doing there?" "Were he and Nicole lovers?"

I could tell you stories like these, but I won't. Instead, I will take you behind the scenes of ten other American tragedies, from as early as the 1960s, when the news consisted of three channels—NBC, ABC, and CBS—and a handful of prominent newspapers and magazines—the *Chicago Tribune,* the *Washington Post,* the *New York Times, LIFE, Time, Vanity Fair*—to as late as today, in 2015, when news outlets and social media sites are too numerous to count. We will spend time with the families themselves, whose lives were featured in hundreds of headlines, news shows, and articles. You know these families. We all do.

We were introduced to them in their most vulnerable moments, when they were experiencing the worst days of their lives.

You watched her collapse to the ground when she realized her six-year-old baby was in *that* classroom in Newtown.

You heard her scream, the kind that surges from the gut, when law enforcement confirmed her daughter had purchased a ticket to the doomed midnight showing of *The Dark Knight Rises* in Aurora.

You may have been skeptical when she said she didn't know why her husband would shoot those little Amish girls.

You might have even seen news clips of them weeping with joy and relief when the parole board denied freedom to Charles Manson and his followers.

You sent these families messages of love. You sent them letters of encouragement—and in some cases, hate. You talked about them at the dinner table, over the water cooler, on Facebook and Twitter, as if they were the new reality show everyone's watching. But you also related to them; you had so much compassion for them. It felt like you knew their pain. But did you, really? *Do you really know what they were experiencing when the cameras weren't rolling?*

I'll take you there, beyond the mass media coverage, for an exclusive glimpse inside their lives—on their terms. Why? Because I think there are some things you need to know.

It's been twenty years since my quiet life was hijacked and I was thrown into the chaotic world known to many as the "Trial of the Century." And every year since, I've watched cable news, newspapers, magazines, the internet, and social media replay to a new generation pivotal moments in the horror that was our daily life, highlighting each painful memory for people to debate and judge. *Did the glove really fit? Was there an accomplice? Was the detective really a racist?* This story, my family story, lives on forever ... with every click of the mouse.

I have often wondered: Did the intense media coverage impede our ability to mourn the loss of my brother, or did having so much support comfort us? Sometimes I think the global hug we received helped us in our darkest hours; I never felt alone. But I also *never felt alone*; wherever I went, the media coverage, the support, the scrutiny—all of it—followed.

I knew I couldn't be the only one concerned with how a family heals when so much attention is focused on them during their grieving process. So I set out to find others with a similar existence and ask them the same question: Did their experiences with the media interrupt their healing or did they feel comforted by it?

I spent hours talking to, and sometimes sitting with, central figures in some of the most notorious crimes of the past few decades. Their chilling but inspiring stories took me back to 1998, when we first heard about a young man beaten and left for dead in Laramie, Wyoming, because he was gay; to 2006 when a cold-blooded sniper terrorized the DC area; and more recently to 2012 when the world was shocked by the revelation that a missing sixteen-year-old girl had been killed by her two best friends.

These brave families let me into their hearts and told me things they've never told anyone else—because I am not a reporter, because we share a deep understanding. However unique the circumstances of our losses, we're all now living a "new normal"—a very different version of who we were seconds before our loved ones were brutally killed at the hands of another.

After that moment, life would never be the same again. And for the rest of our days, we are forced to adjust to it—not alone, with the privacy of family and friends, but in the spotlight, as the country mourns with us; as in the case of Eric Garner's family, who can't escape the public chants of Eric's dying words, *I can't breathe*, everywhere they turn.

So many of the people featured in this book said to me, "the reporters are just doing their jobs." Just doing their job as they stick microphones in our faces, asking "How are you feeling?" as we race from the driveway to our house, just minutes after planning a funeral. When does it cross the line and become unnecessary and inappropriate? And whose responsibility is it to hold the media and the public to a standard that includes boundaries and sensitivity?

The media's ultimate goal is supposed to be telling a story that is well rounded, informative, and objective—right? And in order to achieve that, sometimes reporters go to great lengths, leaving no stone unturned—even finding stories where there isn't one. They aren't thinking about what gets left in their wake because their agenda is often different than ours, the victims. And yet we are forced together by an unfortunate circumstance. How do we make this unwanted relationship work?

The families profiled in this book told me that they've come to understand the role of the reporter, but I wonder: Has anyone in the newsrooms ever thought about what it is like to live a private tragedy in the public eye? Have their readers?

Since Ron and Nicole's murder, I have had the incredible opportunity to travel the country, meeting other victims and survivors, learning their stories, and then sharing their experiences with those who have the power to better assist them. I have spoken at numerous victims' rights events, advocating for fairer treatment of victims in the courtroom; I've provided countless sensitivity training sessions for law enforcement, served as a panelist discussing ethics in media and the role of the reporter when covering high-profile cases, and so much more. And so one of the main reasons I wanted to write this book was to remind others, the public and the media, that behind every story is a human being, deserving of decency, respect, and honor.

I wanted to help sensitize a culture that I strongly believe has become, at times, numb to the pain and anguish of others, contributing to our overwhelming sense of apathy toward one another.

Yes, that is a sweeping generalization, but I have seen firsthand the negativity, hate, and hostility that can ferment on the internet due to a lack of understanding and compassion—a disconnect between a headline and the family behind it. In fact, several of the participants in this book share stories of being on the receiving end of that hurtful behavior.

The twenty-four-hour news cycle creates a need for content that can drive members of the media to sometimes act irresponsibly in their reporting, because they are competing with the amateur journalists that pop up on every blog and every corner of the internet. It also creates a false sense of connectedness. The constant barrage and endless replay of information creates the illusion that you can have access to anyone and anything in an instant, right at your fingertips. And even though the tragedies the media shares with us readers and viewers didn't happen to us, we take them on as if they did—the loss, the anger, the love, the injustice. We feel it, deeply. And then, just like that, we move onto the next big story, leaving behind a family in turmoil.

Have we become confused about the line between "the public's right to know" and an invasion of privacy? Have we come to believe that just because a story is on our feed, we are obligated to share, comment, like, repost, or retweet? Do we ever ask ourselves *why* we do it? And *who* we are affecting when we do?

The families in this book have come to terms with their place in history, but that acceptance is the end point of a journey laced with pain. The way the media descends on a bereaved family in crisis can steal away their grief. Catapulting a family, fresh in mourning, in front of the cameras can be cruel and invasive. But sometimes the subtler cruelty is in the lingering effects of inaccurate information, rumors about the dead, and assumptions and debates about issues that have little to do with why the person was murdered. This is not a book of criticisms but of lessons, for all of us—for victims and survivors, for the media, and for readers.

These stories of heartbreak and hope, from some very familiar faces, provide a fresh look at stories that you think you know. I hope that after reading them, the next time you hear a story about a violent murder or see a news report on a missing child, you'll wonder: What would it be like to walk a mile in that person's headlines?

And I hope you never look at the media circus the same way again.

DEBRA TATE

Sister of Charles Manson
murder victim Sharon Tate

August 9, 1969

Top left: Debra, July 1969, just weeks before Sharon's murder. *Center right:* Debra, 2014, in Palm Springs promoting her book *Sharon Tate: Recollection.* *Center left:* Sharon, age ten, and Debra, age six months. *Bottom right:* Sharon, Debra, and Roman Polanski, 1967.

I first met Debra Tate, the younger sister of murdered actress Sharon Tate, on *Larry King Live* back in 2010. We were there to talk about the Los Angeles Police Department's plan to display artifacts from our siblings' slayings in an exhibition, titled "Behind the Scenes, the LAPD Homicide Exhibit." Both of us expressed our dismay over the LAPD's lack of sensitivity in not notifying us in advance of its plans. We were two sisters, sitting side by side, still fighting with our grief so many years after our siblings' brutal deaths. I was both empowered and saddened. But in that moment, a special relationship was born.

We don't know much about each other on a personal level, but the empathy we feel toward one another is deep. We've touched base a handful of times throughout the years via email or text, always signing off, "Sister to Sister, XO." So when we reconnected recently for this book, in a stunning art-deco style loft in downtown Los Angeles, home to one of Debra's good friends, the conversation just flowed, as if we had spoken every day for the last twenty years.

Like me, Debra grew up in the public eye and in and out of courtrooms. We were both so young when one of the worst things that could ever happen happened to us: I was just twenty-two and Debra was only sixteen.

I had come to hear Debra's story in depth, knowing that the Charles Manson murders was one of the very first crime cases in modern times that captured the public's imagination, setting the standard for how the media would cover ordinary people associated with subsequent high-profile crimes and murder trials.

There was no setup, no pleasantries before Debra began to tell me her story—just a warm hug and, as she spoke, plenty of head nods, affirmations, and tears.

"My boyfriend Wayne called our Palos Verdes home, and told Mother that he had heard about my sister Sharon on a radio program."

That morning it was falsely reported that there was a fire at the Benedict Canyon house, rumored to be the home of actress Sharon Tate, where she and four others perished.

"Mother, my younger sister Patti, and myself had just moved back from the Presidio military base in San Francisco, where we'd been living for three years. Dad was still there, finishing up his tour of duty. It was so hot that day, and we'd been unpacking forever. But since my mother had the neighbor over, having coffee cake, I took the opportunity to take a shower, to feel the cold water on my skin.

"Suddenly, Mother came bursting into the bathroom, supported by the neighbor woman, because her knees were buckling; she just threw the shower door open and told me that Sharon was dead and then she collapsed. I told the neighbor to take her back to the kitchen. I got out of the shower without even rinsing the soap from my hair, wrapped in a towel, ran down the hall leaving a trail of water behind me, and asked my mother to explain herself to me again."

With her mother breaking down in front of her, and her father far away, all Debra had was her gut. She knew she needed to get answers.

"I phoned Wayne and asked him to tell me the radio station he was listening to. I called the station and asked them to reiterate the story to me. I was told it was a fire. So I called the Beverly Hills Fire Department but they said there was no report of a fire at that address. They suggested that I call the police instead. It took me awhile to get to the right precinct, but I did.

"At that time, they told me that there was an incident, but they wouldn't tell me what the incident was, exactly. Of course they had asked me who I was, and what my relationship was to Sharon. They wanted to know my age, and I said sixteen. We went back and forth several times until the detectives realized that I was the only reasonable person at that point to tell."

Police never went to Debra's family's house, and reporters did not think to call them, either, before airing the horrific news for the world to hear.

"There was no policy back then, like now, where you have to make first-of-kin notification before releasing identity," Debra said.

The Tate case was different than anything else in the news at that time: During a period when war and racial strife dominated the television and newspapers, the story of a beautiful, twenty-six-year-old actress and a charismatic serial killer gripped audiences and catapulted an ordinary family into the spotlight. The fact that Sharon Tate was married to acclaimed film director Roman Polanski and was eight months pregnant no doubt contributed to the public interest.

"I really think that this is the first case where the media spun out of control," Debra said.

But while this story might have captured the nation's imagination, what happened that night on 10050 Cielo Drive was very real for the Tate family.

Polanski was in London at the time, so Sharon had invited friends to the rented home, a beautiful French-country estate that stood on three acres and had been previously rented by other Hollywood types, such as Cary Grant and Henry Fonda.

On the evening of August 8, 1969, Sharon had returned to her residence at 10:30 p.m., after having dinner at El Coyote in Los Angeles with friends Jay Sebring, a thirty-five-year-old Hollywood hairstylist; Abigail Folger, the twenty-five-year-old coffee heiress; and Folger's boyfriend, thirty-two-year-old Voytek Frykowski, a writer and friend of Roman's.

Shortly after 8 a.m. the next morning, the maid entered the home as she normally would, but quickly rushed out screaming, "Murder, death, bodies, blood!"

When police officers arrived at the scene, they immediately found the body of Steve Parent still seated in the driver's side of his father's car.

Only eighteen years old, Parent had come to the home to visit the nineteen-year-old caretaker, William Garretson, and was the first to die in the ambush when he was shot four times in the arm, face, and chest while waiting at the estate's gate to exit; unfortunately for him, his visit was ending at the same exact moment Manson followers, called "The Family," were creeping onto the grounds.

The bodies of Sharon and Sebring were discovered in the living room, a nylon rope tied around their necks, connecting them. Sharon had been stabbed sixteen times. Sebring had been shot and stabbed seven times. Folger was able to flee the house, but was tackled on the front lawn and stabbed twenty-eight times. Frykowski, who fought the hardest, also made it outside the house despite being shot. Police found his mutilated body on the lawn; he had been beaten on the head eighteen times, stabbed fifty-one times, and shot twice.

The young caretaker was the sole survivor. He was immediately taken into custody as LAPD's chief suspect, but was eventually cleared of any wrongdoing. Later, it was learned that his life was spared only because Patricia Krenwinkel, one of Manson's followers, didn't check the cottage where he was living.

When an officer called in five homicides in Bel Air, the media listening in on the scanners rushed to the scene. I watched old news footage of a press conference held that morning: at least fifteen television, newspaper, and radio reporters, photographers, and cameramen, all of them male, surround a police lieutenant at the scene of the crime. The reporters rattle off a burst of questions:

"Was anyone hung?"

"Was someone mutilated?"

"Was there something scrawled on the front door in blood?"

"I can't tell you," the lieutenant said. "We are still conducting an investigation."

"Was she pregnant?"

The lieutenant answers, "Yes, she is, but I won't discuss the details."

Unlike today, there was no public relations representative to address the media's questions, and there wasn't a large group of officials standing together behind a podium with talking points, controlling the message. The news footage shows reporters standing outside the house where the murders occurred, right next to the car where one of the victims was killed hours earlier.

The police lieutenant—clearly trying to answer each question with as little information as he can, despite how much knowledge the reporters already seem to have—remains cordial and patient. Overall though, he just looks *stunned* by the media frenzy, a tame precursor of a scene that has become too familiar today.

"Once I got ahold of Father," Debra said, "he got in his car and drove home, and went immediately to the crime scene—until he did that, we did not know any of the gruesome details.

"To the best of my knowledge, the first pictures that were released were in the early morning news the next day."

And then she recalled Sharon's funeral.

"My mom and Roman, Sharon's husband, exited right in front of me and a cameraman actually knocked me over and bloodied my knees and tore my stockings; I went down on all fours, onto the palms of my hand, just so someone could get a picture. It was a television camera guy. He had the giant thing on his shoulder so I tripped that son of a bitch."

The place was packed; it was an A-list funeral

"Everybody in Hollywood, every star from all over the world was there. That day was really weird. I am sure, Kim, you experienced it too; it was almost out-of-body. You're robotic, you're going through the motions and there's a dialogue going through your head but the dialogue isn't present in this mind," she says, tapping on her temple. "It's like hovering from out here, talking you through the whole process."

In the days after the murder and funeral Debra quickly found herself scrambling to care for her family.

"I had been accepted as an equal into Sharon's world. I was hanging out with people ten years my senior. So I was very mature. I was really well organized in my brain, but this just knocked everything out of the box and my head struggled to put the building blocks back together. But it was urgent for me to figure it out, especially for my little sister, Patti."

Being the daughter of a high-ranking military officer, she was used to living all over the world, and to keeping her family in order. "I was the one that would be responsible for packing up the house as we moved from country to country. My mother was busy doing the officer's wife thing and the teas and the cocktail parties—you know, the whole thing that goes on with high-powered officers' wives—and Sharon was my rock then."

So it was left up to Debra to care for Patti, who was just twelve at the time, in a home where her father, as Debra explained, shut down completely after Sharon's death, and her mother fell into a very dark depression.

"No young person should be left to do this. But you do what you have to do for the greater good of taking care of the family. You deal with all the rest of it as it comes, and try not to analyze it too much. And for me, Kim, I did not object to it too much. I knew that there was nothing that I could do but put one foot in front of the other, and move forward."

As Debra was adjusting to her new role within the family, the Los Angeles newspapers and television stations were broadcasting and publishing nonstop coverage. Some locals believed that certain articles contributed to the fear and paranoia that followed the crimes, with headlines such as "LA Manhunt Widens; Two Others Slain," "Film Star Stabbed in 'Ritualistic' Killings," and "Sadist Hunted in 7 Murders."

Polanski was highly criticized for participating in a *Life* magazine feature that showed him standing next to the front door with the word "Pig" still present and written in his wife's blood. He responded by explaining that he just wanted to shock the public into calling police with information, if they knew something.

Polanski also blew up at the media during a press conference, complaining that reporters focused too much on Sharon's looks and not her as a person. Meanwhile, the parents of Steve Parent, the young man killed as he was leaving the estate, complained the media focused only on the famous victims and had forgotten about their son.

The media spotlight was obviously getting to the people close to the case. I wondered how prepared Debra and her family were for all of the public attention that had only been directed at Sharon before.

"Sharon and Roman's life was already very public and they had their moments when the whole world was watching. They had a friend, a photographer, who practically lived with them; there would always be a camera, a still camera, following and photographing and documenting their life. With the success of *Valley of the Dolls*, their wedding, and with *Rosemary's Baby* about to be released, they were used to dealing with spurts of publicity, but you still have some of your privacy back at home. *We* weren't ready at all for the media circus that was to follow her death."

Today's press can be pushy, invasive, and sensational, but I imagined the media back then being more supportive and kind to the Tate family.

"Rude, all of them," Debra quickly remarked. Not just the press, she explained, but their audiences, too. "Some of the general public would just come by and leave a card and some little cookies in a tin—some of them were very nice. But some of them were very pushy, like making you feel like a freak. And the media were just intrusive and gawking. Their questions were rude and terribly insensitive."

Debra told me the reporters and photographers would camp out right outside their home.

"And if they came up to the driveway we had to push them back to the sidewalk and the street. The news trucks and the looky-loos, it was a three-ring circus, the phone was constantly ringing, it was crazy."

This would be just the beginning to a lifelong legacy of "crazy" for the Tate family. It took three months before anyone would be arrested for the horrific murders, but those three months were torture for the residents of the city's most affluent enclaves.

Dominick Dunne, the late Hollywood producer, *Vanity Fair* scribe, and friend to me during my brother's murder trial, reflected back on the experience years later. "The shock waves that went through the town were beyond anything I had ever seen before. People were convinced that the rich and famous of the community were in peril. Children were sent out of town. Guards were hired."

Dubbing the killings simply the "Tate murders," the press had become completely fascinated by the crime, and by Sharon, who in death was front-page news for weeks, though in life the gorgeous actress was only on the brink of becoming a Hollywood "it girl." She had appeared on *The Beverly Hillbillies* and *Petticoat Junction* and was nominated for a Golden Globe for her role in *Valley of the Dolls*, but she hadn't yet emerged as a huge star.

Even during a year packed with monumental events—the gruesome murders stood out above the Woodstock music festival in New York, the Apollo 11 moon landing, and the tragedy in Chappaquiddick, where US Senator Ted Kennedy accidentally drove his car off a tidal channel, killing his young female passenger.

It's been described as "the defining moment of the sixties," the one that put an end to the free-love hippie movement. And it's still a story the country continues to be fixated on.

"Anybody that comes into my house is curious. People like to talk to you on the phone because they're talking to 'Debra Tate.'

There's still that morbid curiosity and they want to see what kind of person you are, or try to get in your head a little bit."

But somewhere down the line, maybe during the Manson Family's over-the-top court appearances, the media interest switched from Sharon Tate to Manson, the thirty-five-year-old fringe musician and drifter whose eerie control over his followers transformed a group of hippies into serial killers. Manson believed the murders would set off an apocalyptic race war called "Helter Skelter," the name borrowed from a Beatles' song, leaving him in a position of power.

Second to everyone's fascination with Manson was the celebrity element to the story beyond Polanski and Tate. Manson wasn't targeting Tate and her friends, but chose the house because it was where record producer Terry Melcher, the son of Doris Day, once lived with actress Candice Bergen. Manson, who had been at the home before, was angry at Melcher, who had changed his mind about producing some of Manson's songs.

The local papers in Los Angeles competed to see who could attract more readers with the most sensational Manson stories. The national media was also in the game, sending legions of reporters and photographers to West Virginia to find anything they could on Manson's childhood.

Manson hasn't been a free man since 1971, but he has never really disappeared from public consciousness, either. He has been featured in books, movies, documentaries—even headlines, as in 2014 when he received a license from prison to marry a twenty-six-year-old woman. All that attention begot a whole new generation of Manson followers, which might seem harmless to some, but not to Debra.

"I have at least three, four, up to five death threats a year from Manson's second wave of followers. I'm sure he probably doesn't know who they are but he has followers and he knows that. Each of them has their own private group as well as the main group," she said. "Charlie has over 80,000 likes on Facebook now. He's also hooked up with the Aryan Brotherhood. There is an army waiting for him. Frustrating—the whole damn thing."

She didn't look scared, but how could she not feel fear?

"I live behind gates, thick gates. I have my haters. It is just human nature. I don't know why. But yes, a majority of the public are still supportive and loving and kind."

Still, I couldn't help but feel that underneath her tough exterior, behind the feistiness that she attributes to being a natural redhead, that she is still that teenage girl who lost so much of her innocence to death and despair.

"It's very lonely, this life," she admits, "but we're here for a reason."

Being victims and survivors, we do walk the line between being guarded, for fear of not wanting to get hurt if we let people get close to us, but staying as open as we can, because we want to be connected and loved. We've looked evil in the eye, we've seen it firsthand. So how do we remain hopeful? How does Debra trust people, trust their intentions?

"For me I always want to remain trusting because part of my spiritual belief is that we should be open with the heart of the child, and if you are, good things will come to you," she told me. "That doesn't mean that your life is going to be a bowl of cherries. It does mean that if you are open and quiet that even the *ugly* things that come to you are a wonderful lesson and a gift. I work very hard at keeping my heart open; they [the killers] rule the day when they take that away from me."

She told me that through this entire experience, she found solace in helping others. It started with her little sister Patti and the role Debra assumed as caretaker when Sharon died. "She was my immediate focus—it was not on myself but on Patti. I was trying to be some kind of pillar of strength, amidst the chaos. And that's why I never cried back then, because I had to be the pillar."

But it didn't stop there. Debra and her family became pioneers in the victims' movement after Sharon's death. At different times in their lives, Patti, her mother Doris, and Debra all played significant roles. In fact, Doris, after battling depression, found her purpose and became an integral member of a group that worked diligently on California Proposition 8, the Victims' Bill of Rights, which was passed in 1982.

Proposition 8 allowed crime victims the opportunity to speak in court, by reading a "victim impact statement" during the sentencing phase of the criminal trial. Doris became the first Californian to make such a statement after the law was passed, when she spoke at the parole hearing of one of her daughter's killers.

Debra's family was also committed to attending every Manson Family parole hearing, protesting against their release. While most of Debra's family members are now gone, she's still keeping up the fight for them.

Despite all her hard work to keep her sister's killers behind bars, there are still those people, most of them Manson groupies, who are opposed to what she is doing.

"But would those same people want one of those idiots [Manson's followers] living next door to them? Because that's exactly what's going to happen if I stop fighting," she said. "I'm not doing this for *my* family—it's not going to bring Sharon or the others back or change any of my history—but it might change yours."

She told me that, during the parole hearings, she shares every grisly detail of each victim's death, describing what was done to them. "I am very graphic. Those wounds are on our hearts and in our souls for the rest of our lives. I want the parole judges to look into my eyes and feel the pain."

She wishes the people who rally against her could do the same. "This is real, this isn't a fictional story, this isn't an abstract— so let me take you through it: *The knife went here and went in this deep* . . . So yeah, you can get real graphic and sometimes you have to make these people *feel*, because once again the media has desensitized us; sometimes it takes a slap across the face to bring people back to reality."

Thankfully the phone rang right then, and Debra let out a chuckle. I think we both needed a chance to breathe.

Today, Debra is sixty-two years old, still a pretty woman, with long red hair, flawless skin, and hazel eyes, sharing the same model looks as her late sister. But she has worked so hard over the last forty-five years since Sharon's death, you can see the exhaustion etched on her face. She always wanted her sister to be remembered for something other than the way she died, and as the years passed, social media granted her that wish. A new generation of young fans has discovered Sharon, admiring her style and beauty.

But Debra also recalled her experiences with the dark and ugly side of social media.

"My daughter was about fifteen and that's when it became real for her. One of her friends sent her the death scene photos from that night. While she's doing her homework, she gets IM'd and all of a sudden, the main death scene pops up on her computer and she flipped over in the chair from shock. When she got up, her life had changed completely. She was crying. 'Mom, she looked so much like you.' She knew everything, but at that point neither of us had ever looked at the death photos. That was hard."

I knew exactly how she felt; I've had that same worry for my own son, who may someday come across grisly photos of his dead uncle, without being prepared. The access that the internet provides is scary, and it's not ours to control. And even though I speak graphically about Ron's murder, having strangers see pictures of his mutilated body, without me being present, makes me feel violated.

Debra told me she doesn't see it as a violation to her personally. "I just don't want anyone to see Sharon's or Jay's or Abigail's, or Ron's or anyone's, lifeless bodies. That is *their* most private moment, when they are most vulnerable; they can't do anything about it. That should be something that should be reserved for us and them; it's a very intimate moment."

Even though she has devoted her life to victims' rights, she does not feel the need to follow other high-profile crimes that have become entertainment for many people nowadays.

"I know I have very little faith in our legal system at this point and even back then, I realized that there are 'spins' that are put on things. So I think it's kind of pointless to watch the details. I am certainly aware of the fact that everything is being vented to the public and I feel resentful at that moment for the actual families going through it."

And yet, she can still appreciate how these stories are riveting to the viewer and how easy it is to become consumed with every facet of the story.

"Even someone as sensitive as you and I do it," she said to me. "I'm sure as fast as it comes out in the news, you look for a second and go, 'Oh my God—wait a minute, I'm part of the problem, change the channel.'"

Debra says her relationship with the media has evolved since the days she got knocked around by photographers at her sister's funeral.

"It's love/hate."

On the more negative end: "I won't let reporters into my home because every time a crew came in, something walked out with them." She also dislikes the lies and untruths journalists often fed to the public. "If they didn't have the whole story, then they would just make something up," she shared. "Yes, I had great resentment for them."

So she had to learn how to handle herself and the media's questions.

"Some of them are insensitive, but that is their job, to want to make the story as sensational as possible so it makes the news, so it makes the air."

But she also knows the media can be her biggest ally, when she needs the public to pay attention during her many trips to Central California's Corcoran State Prison to remind the board of the depraved and villainous ways of Manson and his followers, who were all sentenced to life in prison.

Her efforts have proved successful, so far: Charles Manson has been denied parole twelve times, Susan Atkins eighteen times, and Charles "Tex" Watson fourteen times. Patricia Krenwinkel was told no thirteen times, while the parole board slammed the door shut on Leslie Van Houten twenty times.

"To do that, I know the media is my best tool. So I had to tweak and adjust my gut emotions, in order to make it all work."

MILDRED MUHAMMAD

Ex-wife of the DC Sniper

October 2–22, 2002

Top left: Mildred. *Top right:* A recent photo of Mildred and her children (from left to right: Salena, Lil John, and Taalibah). *Bottom:* Mildred and her ex-husband, DC Sniper John Muhammad, with one of their three children.

Prior to speaking to Mildred Muhammad, I did my homework. I read articles about her and watched her on an old CNN clip of *Larry King Live*. I kept thinking, she has such a sense of self—she's so smart, so in the moment. As I watched the interview a little more, I couldn't help but think that Larry was tiptoeing around her. She seemed like she had so much to say but was holding something inside.

I thought back to those eighteen chaotic days in October 2002, when a ruthless sniper stalked the US Capitol. People were terrified, walking zigzag down the street, cowering as they pumped gas and ducking into buildings. By the time the sniper was done terrorizing the nation, ten seemingly random people had been executed and three wounded by the man the media deemed the Beltway Sniper, also known as the DC Sniper.

Mildred, too, was looking over her shoulder during that time, but for two different people: the Beltway Sniper and her husband, John. She had no idea they were one in the same.

From the moment we said hello, Mildred and I clicked. She laid out the ground rules for the rest of our interview early: "Ask any question you want, I have heard it all," she said. "You don't have to walk on eggshells."

I liked her already.

I began by sharing a little bit about myself and my experiences with the media and the public, wondering if she'd experienced the same. I shared how some people treated me with respect during my brother and Nicole's murder trial and others acted the exact opposite.

"Sometimes," I told her, "people are like 'Oh Kim, you poor thing . . .'"

She interrupted. "They never said that to me."

Mildred was quiet for a long time. I could tell she was think-ing. I would later learn the silence was intentional. Her voice was calm and confident when she spoke again. "I listened to every word you said about what happened to you and your family, from the media being hurtful and people being mean and hateful, to those people who were kind and compassionate. I didn't get any of that. I didn't get any kindness from anybody. I didn't get any support from anybody."

It hit me just how different Mildred's story is from that of most survivors I've talked to, and from my own story. Although her husband emotionally abused her for years, kidnapped her children for eighteen months, and executed a bloody, elaborate rampage in order to conceal that she was the intended target, Mildred was never looked at as a victim, just as the wife of a mass murderer.

It's not like she'd never told anyone about how dangerous her husband was. In fact, it was just the opposite. Long before her ex-husband began killing innocent people, she'd tell anyone with ears: the police, the FBI, friends, family, social service agencies, even a local radio station. But no one listened to her because he never physically attacked her. Not even her friends could conceive that the charming man they knew, the loving father, was really a monster.

The heartbreaking part? "Kim, if they had listened to me, those people would be alive today."

Mildred's nightmare began when John returned from the Gulf War in the late nineties. Once jovial, he was now a different man: withdrawn, bitter, and angry at the military, at her, at the world.

"He was a combat engineer, a demolition expert. But John took his job from the military and brought it to the civilian sector."

Although he was a caring and attentive father, he created rigid rules, was demanding, manipulative, inattentive toward Mildred, and was very secretive. Always the dutiful wife, she endured the emotional games, the string of affairs, and his odd behavior. He'd take mysterious night rides on a bicycle he painted black, and habitually did away with household goods such as plates, cups, and knives.

After she told John she wanted a divorce, he repeatedly changed her phone number, so no one could call her, and he'd break into the house in the middle of the night, standing over while she pretended to sleep. He began to withhold money that Mildred, their children, and Mildred's mother, who was living with them at the time, needed for groceries.

Everything came to a head during a confrontation in their garage in 2000. "He told me, 'You have become my enemy and as my enemy I will kill you.' And I knew that he was going to carry that out. I knew he would kill me and put me somewhere that no one would be able to find me. I knew John."

Since he was an expert gunman, she also understood it would be "one shot to the head."

Fully aware that John didn't make idle threats, she took matters in her own hands, by filing and obtaining a lifelong restraining order and beginning divorce proceedings. During that same month, John and their three children "Lil John," Salena, and Taalibah vanished.

"He kidnapped our children, took them to Antigua, emptied the bank accounts, and left me and my mother penniless."

Three months later, on Mother's Day, Mildred fainted, and was rushed to the hospital, where a doctor told her she had been losing too much blood during her monthly cycle and needed a blood transfusion. As she lay in the hospital, John, still with the children, called and threatened her. Terrified, Mildred immediately called police and fled to a shelter for abused women in Tacoma, Washington, near where they lived.

"I lived in a shelter for eight months. My sister had to come from Maryland to get my mother to go live with her. Nobody knew where I was for months. I was completely in hiding."

She lived her life in constant fear, changed her name, and wore a disguise every time she walked out the door. She knew if she wanted to find her children, she needed to learn to navigate the legal system. First, she took a mail-order correspondence course to become a paralegal. She then interned at the YWCA's legal department and became a certified domestic violence advocate, which meant she answered phone calls, placed the victims' names in a database, and sometimes, still in disguise, accompanied the victims to court. All of this helped her complete her own parenting plan, prepare for custody hearings, finalize her divorce, and write and file the necessary paperwork to get her children back.

The hard work paid off. Eighteen months after John and their three children disappeared, Mildred, who'd just moved to Maryland to live with her sister and brother-in-law, received a phone call. Her children had been found.

On September 5, 2001, she was reunited with them in Washington State, where John had been detained after he returned to the country with the children.

On the final day of their custody hearing, John walked up to Mildred, her attorney, and one of her close friends in court and mouthed, "Gotcha."

She knew what he meant: This war was not over, and he'd be the victor.

Realizing she was a marked woman, that night Mildred fled again, this time with her three children, back to Maryland with her sister and brother-in-law. Luckily, John didn't know her brother-in-law's last name or where he lived.

Residing in a quiet suburb of Maryland, Mildred found a job and good schools and she was able to reacquaint herself with her children. Life was becoming calm again—until police showed up at her door on October 23, 2002. They needed her to come with them to the police department, where an FBI agent told her the unthinkable. The authorities suspected her ex-husband was the notorious DC Sniper. Mildred was shocked.

Like the rest of the country, she had been terrified to hear on the news that there was a spree of shootings in the area, several of them close to her home. It had only been a year since she had reunited with her children, and she was unaware that her husband had been hunting her down for months.

A blue car parked near her home hadn't given her too much pause because she was keeping her eye out for the mysterious sniper and his white van, as reported in the news. But John's seventeen-year-old accomplice, Lee Boyd Malvo, later would say he was behind the wheel of the blue car and the man sitting in the passenger seat, who hid his face with a newspaper . . . was John.

Mildred had known John wanted *her* dead, but never did she think he'd kill innocent people. So when the FBI agent told her the news on October 23, "I was in total disbelief." Then, she remembered something: John had once bragged that he had the skills to terrorize an entire city.

Suddenly, disbelief turned into fear. "They didn't know John. I knew him. I was scared for my life."

Mildred needed to get home; police were ready to put her entire family into protective custody, including her three children, her sister, and her brother-in-law. She rushed out of the police station parking lot, passing a convoy of media trucks just pulling into the lot.

The next day, while the family ate breakfast and watched the news in a Maryland hotel, they learned that John and Malvo had been captured and arrested.

It was a surreal moment. In tears, the children witnessed the entire drama unfolding on television, all the world watching along with them.

As frustrated as Mildred was with the media in the days that followed, the constant news coverage kept her informed. Every day she learned something new about the man she thought she'd known better than anyone in the world. She was surprised to discover John was making a living falsifying documents and identification cards for people from the Caribbean, to be smuggled into the United States. Most shocking to her was learning that Malvo and John were responsible for the death of twenty-one-year-old Keenya Cook, the niece of Mildred's best friend, Isa Nichols, who had helped Mildred escape Tacoma in September 2001.

Malvo would later testify that John sent him to kill Isa at her home in Tacoma on February 16, 2002, but Malvo froze and shot point-blank the first person who opened the door.

I wondered, did Mildred try to shield her kids from the minute-by-minute broadcasts and all the "breaking news" about their father? What she told me was surprising.

"My children were eight, nine, and eleven. When they came home from school, we talked about it," she said. "That's how I shielded them. I told them what was going on in the news; I told them we were going to watch this newscast for some piece of new information coming out, and then we would sit down and talk about it."

One of the things Mildred learned from media was that it was John's best friend, Robert, who called the FBI and said he thought he knew who the sniper was.

"He told them that he didn't know anything about their case, but that they might want to look at John Allen Muhammad, because his ex-wife is in the area and he may be there to hurt her."

When Mildred heard about Robert's telephone call to police, she called to thank him for saving her life.

"He said, 'Let me tell you something. Don't get it twisted. You know John is my friend and I love him to death. I knew that was him shooting people. I did not want to see your name scrolling at the bottom of that TV. That's why I made the call. Regardless of what they tell you and what anybody does, John came there to kill you. That was the plan that he set up and you were going to die that day. It was going to be a headshot. A one shot, one kill.'"

Robert's call changed the course of the investigation and soon after the information was released to the media it catapulted

Mildred into the media spotlight. "That's when everyone started looking at me. But police started to look at me in a manner where they tried to make me a part of it."

ABC was the first media outlet to call on her, promising to put her family up in a hotel for months if she wanted, for her continued safety. Meanwhile, she got word that she couldn't go home to her sister's house because the media trucks were waiting there. Soon, dozens of news organizations were calling her cell phone.

In my own case, I remembered watching the news or reading articles, and being aghast at the difference between the truth and the media's version of it. Did she witness the media trying to "spin" her story, too?

"Yes," Mildred told me, but she wasn't going to let them do it. The most important thing to her was to maintain the integrity of her story.

She shared that one tabloid promised to pay her $65,000 if she gave them an interview. Financially strapped, she agreed and sat down for questions, but declined to falsely claim that John wanted to kill the president.

"They wanted me to lie," she said. "First of all, I'm not going to lie." She never got a penny.

"There was another media group that wanted me to walk around the areas where the victims had been shot. I said no. Then they said, 'Well you are a Muslim, we want you to pull out your prayer rug and show you praying.' I said no, I'm not doing that."

Mildred knew they were trying to exploit her, and she told them just that. "They said, 'Mrs. Muhammad, you just don't want to cooperate.' I said, 'Let me tell you this, you don't have to film me. You know how many survivors want to tell their story? You can pack up your stuff and leave right now. It's not a big deal to me.'"

Another media outlet wanted to use footage of her from a previous television interview for a story they were producing about Lee Malvo, the accomplice.

"I told them no. I think they had five different executive producers call me and I told them all no. And they said, 'Well, we don't understand why you don't want to do this." I said, 'I don't understand why you don't understand no. Is it the *n* or the *o*? Which don't you understand, so I can explain it to you, and you won't keep calling me?"

Soon, one of the top dogs from that same news organization was calling Mildred. "I explained, 'There are three types of victims here: there's Lee Malvo; me and my children; and those ten people killed and three wounded by John. You are trying to thrust me and my children into an area that we do not belong. We do not belong in the area with the victims who were killed. And when you come and try to put us there, you're trying to force us down the throats of these people. And when you leave, you are going to leave all of this trauma behind and you are going to go back to your life and your job. So please stop calling me.'"

She was eventually called upon to testify during John's criminal trial. Finally, she thought the world would know that she had been victimized too—but the prosecution ultimately decided not to use her.

"I only testified in the sentencing phase. My children and I were totally dismissed during the case. My case for domestic violence was not even heard in the trial. So, when I say that we were on the outskirts of all of this, that's what we were. Everything else that happened before the killings was inconsequential."

What bothered Mildred most was when someone would ask, what about the victims?

"I'm thinking in my mind, well, I was a victim too. Are you saying you can only be a victim if you are physically mutilated or if you've been killed?"

The media was just as dismissive. Although, she said, they rightfully were sensitive to the victims' families, especially the children, no one considered how her three children were being impacted.

"In my mind they praised the abuser and they forgot about us, the other victims. That's why everybody knows everything about John, because his story was sensational, and nobody knows anything about us," she said. "Kim, they didn't want to know the backstory."

She was right. I knew virtually nothing of her story. I never knew he had been terrorizing her for years. I never knew how hard she had worked to protect herself and her children. I never knew John's motive: kill all those innocent people, kill Mildred, blame the DC Sniper, and then swoop in as the grieving husband and father to regain custody of the kids. I could only imagine her frustration, but realized I've never seen her shed a tear on television, and I wondered how she held it together. I couldn't keep my emotions in check whenever I talked about my brother or our case. The second I got teary-eyed, I could feel the cameras pushing in. And that's the scene that would get replayed over and over.

Mildred explained to me how she outsmarted those reporters who tried to get her to burst into tears. It was a genius idea, really, and it was the only rule she put in place for herself. She'd count to five before she answered any question. That would allow her time to compose herself before proceeding. It's a tactic she still employs today.

"It gives me the opportunity to think clearly on what I want to say and how I want to say it," she told me. "And I can count to five very slowly. That's how I have been able to maintain control. I am going to give you what you want, but on my terms."

It's a magnificent piece of advice, and one that explained the long pauses during the beginning of our conversation.

Now that so much time has passed, Mildred's feelings toward the media have changed. They treat her with more respect, now that it's well known that she was John's intended target. In fact, during the book tour for her memoir *Scared Silent*, reporters finally wanted to hear *her* story.

But the general public still didn't consider her a victim. Even after John was executed in 2009, and Malvo placed in solitary confinement, Mildred recalled that the public response to her continued to be vitriolic.

During book readings or interviews with journalists, she was especially aware of how people felt about her.

"Some have said, 'How dare you write a book? You're just capitalizing off of his crime.' Others said, 'You should have stayed with him. Then he would have only killed you.'"

Others outwardly told her she was no victim at all.

"The public will rip you up one side and down the other, so I decided all I would say is, 'Thank you for your question,' regardless of how bad the question was and then answer as best I could."

I applauded her, knowing how hard it is to keep a stiff upper lip when people are trying to punch you in the gut.

"When I do speaking engagements I am asked if it is okay to call me the ex-wife of the DC Sniper," she told me. "I say, 'Absolutely,' and they say 'Why doesn't it bother you?' Well, number one, it's not a lie is it? I mean I am his ex-wife and he was the DC Sniper. It's the truth. So whatever it takes to get the people in the seats and for me to make them understand that domestic violence doesn't always have physical scars . . . then let's just do that."

She learned other ways to protect herself and her children from wrong information getting out in the media. "For example, I demand that for documentaries, there has to be a clause in the contract that says my images and the images of my children and my story will not to be used in a way to imply that me or my children are a part of, or knew, that John was going to kill innocent people. Now, who told me to put that in there? Me. I had no legal representative to tell me to include that statement. I said that needs to be in there before I do anything because I know how the media can twist and indirectly suggest something."

I loved that she was not going to let herself be manipulated, or exploited, and quickly learned how to flip the media on its head.

It was Mildred's story to tell, and now she'd be in control of how it was told.

"The wind has shifted," she said. "There are more people who support me, but there are still some who don't feel me or my children are victims. And that's okay. The difference is, now people know I was John's target. They all know the truth now. Now, when they recognize me, the first thing they say is, 'How are the children?'"

But what about Mildred? How did she balance her own emotions, while trying to be strong and brave for those that depended on her?

"I didn't cry in front of the kids. I would tell them I was going to the park, where no one was. And I'd roll up the windows and turn the radio on and scream until my head hurt," she told me. "I would scream and scream and cry until I got it all out. I was there for about an hour and then I would go to a restaurant, wash my face, and put my makeup on, and no one ever know what was up. I never cried in front of people. I'm like that deodorant commercial: 'Never let them see you sweat,' that's my motto."

Although she was able to present a calm demeanor, Mildred knew that her family needed help. Every word written by a reporter or uttered on the evening news about the DC Sniper, and every broadcast of John's face on the television screen threw Mildred's three children for a loop.

If they were going to get even half a shot at living a productive, normal, and happy life, Mildred knew she needed to put them in counseling. The problem? It was impossible for her to find a therapist who didn't want to be famous. "Everybody wanted to be on TV discussing what the DC Sniper's children were doing." So she got resourceful again, just like she did when her children went missing. She went to the library and checked out a book on counseling and helped herself.

"After I read the book, I sat my children down, and told them the ground rules. Everyone will say how they feel."

She told them that no one was to judge the person who was speaking or make them feel they were not entitled to their feelings.

"We started talking about how they felt about their dad. My older two were upset because the younger daughter still loved her dad. They remembered the bad stuff, but the younger one does not remember anything," she recalled. "There was some tension there. I said, 'Taalibah—she's the youngest—is entitled to love her dad the way she wants to love him. You don't have to agree with her, not at all. She's entitled and so are you. You're entitled to be angry with your dad. Can she be angry with you because you're angry with your dad? Absolutely not.'"

And that's how the family worked through it. Mildred told me they had to own their individual feelings. And they had to be responsible for those feelings.

"I told them, 'You will not use your dad as an excuse for failure. That will not be happening to you. You got to give me something better than that. I can't use him; and you can't either.'"

"Damn, woman!" I said. "You sure laid down the law."

I had a feeling that she didn't learn that kind of strength and perseverance just from a book. It had to be an innate part of her core being. When I asked her, "Where did you get that from?" she confirmed my inclination; it's who she is.

But was relying on herself enough support for the whole family? During a time of crisis, therapy is a helpful tool toward healing, I suggested. It made me sad that she was worried about privacy within a therapeutic environment, due to the high profile component of her story. But I had a similar concern once: After my brother was killed, I attended a support group but never returned for a second session, because I didn't feel comfortable sharing my personal feelings when it seemed the whole world was watching and listening to every detail.

"I felt so alone. The only thing I could do, really, was to rely on family and friends," I told her. "And as beautiful as that was—having that level of support—I still felt so isolated, I didn't trust anybody outside our house; people were spying on us and they were recording every move and mannerism, making such horrible assumptions about our mood, our feelings, our thoughts, without ever having asked a question of us."

Mildred listened to me and then empathized, "I too, felt isolated, but my isolation became my friend."

I was not surprised by how Mildred coped—after all, she was a survivor. Sometimes, in moments of crisis, you just do what you need to do, and become who you need to be.

Near the end of our conversation, I asked Mildred to focus on her kids again for a minute. How did their friends treat them? How was school life for them?

Once the public knew John was the DC Sniper, Mildred said, she pulled her children out of school.

"They were being threatened. But then there were those who found out, and are still their friends today. They stuck by them. The ones that did not, I explained to my children that their parents were scared and wanted to protect their children."

She told her kids not to be angry. "Because once their parents feel they are safe, they will probably allow them to come back," she said. "Even if they don't, it's okay. That means they weren't supposed to be with you anyway."

I wondered why her children didn't attend the execution. "I read somewhere they didn't want to," I said.

"They did," she corrected me. "But John would not cooperate. He would not talk on the phone with them. His attorney said it was because he would have had to answer their questions as to why, and it would have unraveled all of the mental work he had done to prepare for the execution."

I'd only known her for a few hours at this point, but I'd already learned that Mildred is a strong and dedicated mother, and I knew she would not have denied those children a chance to say goodbye to their father, no matter her own thoughts on the subject.

She understood it wasn't about her, but it was about doing what was best for them. She did take them to Louisiana for John's funeral. However, the media had no idea they were there. She outsmarted them, yet again, allowing her children to mourn in private.

"Since the children couldn't talk to him, they at least wanted to see him for the last time before he was buried," she said. "I didn't go in; I sat in the parking lot. The media didn't know what my children looked like so they were able to walk right by them without being noticed. Once they were done, I could see that this weight had been lifted from their shoulders. They were good."

As I listened, I worried about the three children, hoping they were now living happy lives.

"My son was diagnosed with multiple sclerosis last year. Took my life in a whole different direction. He was 100 percent disabled. I don't know where it came from," she told me. "I didn't have it. No one on John's side has it. It came out of the blue." Now twenty-five, he has since received medical assistance. "He's able," Mildred told me. "He's working. He's great."

Her daughters, at the time Mildred and I talked, were twenty-one and twenty-two. Both of them majoring in vocal performance, one at Cleveland State and the other one at Baldwin Wallace University.

"They both sing opera in eight different languages. One sings alto; the other one sings soprano," she said.

I was happy to hear they were thriving, though I know the healing process is tough and ongoing.

And what about Mildred? She was fifty-four now, and busy running her foundation, After the Trauma, Inc. As an advocate for victims of domestic violence, she travels all over the nation talking to women who have suffered emotional and physical abuse.

I wondered, had she forgiven John? What did she feel about the concept of forgiveness? I have been under such scrutiny for not forgiving the person who I believe killed my brother; I was curious how she felt.

"My daughter Salena was whimpering on the sofa after it was announced that her dad was dead. I said, 'Honey are you okay?' She said, 'Mom, you don't understand. He was going to kill you.' I said, 'Well honey, you got to let that pain go,' and she said, 'But he was going to kill you!'

"I said, 'Not forgiving someone is going to kill *you*. Why give them that power? Why have them rent out space in your head? They're not even around. Forgiving them does not take them off the hook, it frees you up; it helps you to see and understand your life better. It helps to take away the trauma.'"

Mildred told me she refuses to allow John to have any more of her.

"He's not getting it. So I forgave him and I moved on. I can talk about him; it doesn't bother me. He comes up. I can say his name. He's their dad. If I didn't forgive him, then I would not be able to speak to them about him because I would always be angry," she said. "Life is so short."

For two years, her husband kept her away from her children, and then quietly hunted her down "like an animal."

"I was looking over my shoulder. I couldn't go outside. All I want to do now is laugh and have fun, and I'm just not going to allow anybody to steal my joy ever again, in my life."

JUDY SHEPARD

Mother of gay hate-crime victim Matthew Shepard

October 12, 1998

Top: The Shepard family at Yellowstone National Park, August 1998. From left to right: Logan, Matthew, Judy, and Dennis. *Bottom:* Judy and Dennis Shepard at Martha's Vineyard, 2014.

E very family who's ever had a loved one murdered, and then finds themselves in the media spotlight, wonders, *why*? Even during the midst of all the chaos, they feel a twinge of guilt about why the media is paying attention to their plight, when other families are going through the exact same thing—or worse. In my brother's case, the reason was clear: the defendant was a very famous ex-football player. But on October 7, 1998, when Matthew Shepard was brutally pistol-whipped with the barrel of a .357 Magnum, tied to a fence, and left for dead in the freezing cold in Laramie, Wyoming, he was just a twenty-one-year-old gay, University of Wisconsin freshman, who was only known by friends, family, and classmates.

And yet, his attack would draw world-wide press, marches on Fifth Avenue in Manhattan, rallies in the nation's capitol, parades, vigils, and would inspire novels, plays, books, and songs.

Why Matthew? Part of the answer could be timing. Matthew's death followed the coming out of Ellen DeGeneres in 1997. Ellen telling the world that she was gay was all anyone was talking about at the time. She was warm and non-threatening, and her coming out was supposed to be a sign of cultural change. Many hoped it would be a step toward ending homophobia.

Then Matthew's attack happened.

"This is what I was trying to stop," DeGeneres said tearfully during a large candlelight vigil in DC shortly after Matthew's death. "This is why I did what I did."

The heinous and shocking nature of the crime became the first entry point for many Americans, who had no idea gays were targets of violent crimes.

"Matthew Shepard wasn't the first hate crime," DeGeneres said to the crowd of supporters. "It happens every day. There were 2,500 reported cases this year, but most go unreported because gays and lesbians are still in the closet for fear of this exact thing."

DeGeneres and other speakers on the stage that night mentioned another hate-filled crime that shook America's consciousness only four months earlier. The tragic death of James Byrd Jr. likely heightened America's sensitivity toward hate crimes that year, and may have even contributed to some of the interest in Matthew's case.

On June 7, 1998, Byrd, a forty-nine-year-old black man, was chained by his ankles, tied to the back of a pickup truck, and dragged down an East Texas country road near the town of Jasper.

His head was severed when it hit a culvert, his torso dumped in front of an African-American church. His brain and skull, left on the road, were found intact, a clue to medical experts that Byrd was likely conscious during the whole grisly ordeal. The three perpetrators, two of them known white supremacists, were quickly arrested and tried. One of them has since been executed. The horrific case not only shocked the nation, but years later would help inspire the Matthew Shepard and James Byrd Jr. Crime Prevention Act, also known as the Matthew Shepard Act.

Still, Matthew's mother Judy grappled with why her son's case ended up becoming such a rallying cry for a more inclusive society. Why had *his* story attracted global attention?

"It just sort of took on a life of its own," she told me. "But there were a few things that probably contributed to Matt's story in particular: For one, Matt was blond-haired, blue-eyed; he looked like the boy next door."

The executive director of Judy and her husband Dennis' foundation—who had been a friend of Matt's and was a

Harvard-educated journalist—suggested another theory for why Matt's story caught on so quickly. When he was interviewed for a documentary about Matt called *Matt Shepard is a Friend of Mine,* Judy recalled, he said that people look for a story with interesting characters and an interesting story line and with no outcome.

"We had a gay son who we accepted," she added, "so people were thinking, 'Really, they do?' And then again, I think people during that time period were also tired of reading about and writing about the Bill Clinton and Monica Lewinsky sex scandal. This was something totally different. Plus, there was the fact that Matt was still fighting for his life."

The Shepards never wanted to be in the public eye. Judy, who calls herself an "off-the-scales" introvert, said initially the family tried to avoid the media. Despite their reservations, Judy and Dennis Shepard have become tireless advocates for the LGBT community. Judy herself has become an iconic spokesperson for the movement.

But I wondered, was this something they felt pressure to do? In reality, the reasoning was selfless. Judy told me the couple felt compelled to speak out, even before Matthew took his last breath.

"We thought that it would be a disservice to our son, Matt, and his community, to retreat into the shadows. We were kind of outed, like Matt was outed as a gay man. There was never any question that we would love and support him. There's never any rejection context to Matt's story at all, ever."

Judy, Dennis, and their youngest son, Logan, began to think that if they took this opportunity to show that love and support they had for Matt and his community, then maybe other families would rethink the decision to reject their child or a friend because the person happened to be gay, lesbian, bisexual, or transgender. In December 1998, Dennis and Judy started the Matthew Shepard

Foundation in his memory, to help young people struggling with issues regarding their sexuality.

"We knew it would haunt us, if we didn't take advantage of this opportunity to try to make a difference in another family's life," Judy said. "We loved and accepted our child, and he had been taken from us in act of violence and these folks are giving up their child voluntarily—that's unacceptable."

Matthew's death triggered a national backlash against homophobia, and brought international attention to hate-crime legislation. Productions of *The Laramie Project*, a play of Matthew's life, continue to tour the country. In 2009, President Obama signed the Matthew Shepard Law, making it a federal crime to assault people based on sexual orientation, gender, and gender identity.

The impact of Matthew's death has been tremendous. Survivors are often told to get over it already, just move on, get closure, enough is enough. Yet we don't always have the choice to do that.

On my better days I'm just moving along, living my life, and then suddenly there's a new TV series about Nicole and my brother's murder and the trial. And then all the commentary that follows. I can't even begin to count all of the clever ways the media has tried to link my brother and Nicole's death with some other news story that had no connection to them at all, other than the fact that someone was killed.

I wondered out loud what Judy thought about being forced to relive the tragedy and over and over, every time Matthew's name is mentioned or even a whisper of another gay hate crime reaches her ears.

Her answer surprised and intrigued me.

"I can't complain," she said. "We do relive the tragedies every day in one form of another, whether we do it in front of people or not, but I drive that as much as the media, because I do a lot of lecturing on hate crimes. What I *can* complain about are the people who continue not to tell the truth. I'm talking about those who insert themselves in a high-profile case when it has nothing to do with them."

I knew Judy was talking about an explosive book that came out in 2013. She never really spoke about the book publicly, but I'd read articles about it all over the internet: The author, an investigative journalist, who was himself gay, claimed crystal meth, not Matthew's sexuality, was central to his attack. The book faced a barrage of criticism from gay advocates, but many mainstream media outlets took the book very seriously. Judy definitely had some thoughts about that book.

"It claimed that my son was really a drug dealer and his death was not a hate crime. I wanted to say, 'Don't you think the police investigated that?' It was public knowledge. But time goes by and people forget. They want it to be something different than a hate crime," she said. "I know what happened as much as anyone knows, but really only three people know *exactly* what happened that night, and one of them is dead and will never tell his side and the other two continue to say they didn't know Matt before that night at all."

She told me about someone in the book who the author says was Matt's lover. Supposedly, this mystery man is still wearing Matt's ashes around his neck.

"I have no idea who this person is," Judy said. "Matt never mentioned him. This is like the public's desire to build someone up and you just can't wait to tear them down. And that's what upsets us the most, that we have no control over the stories that people tell, whether it's the truth or a lie."

I told Judy that we've had many books and stories written about our case and everyone involved—I understood the desire to set every record straight, because you want the legacy to be pure. It's not because their *life* was necessarily pure, but because you only want the truth to be linked to their name and story. I asked Judy: How did she counter fabrication in a book that received so much press?

"We ignored it," she said. "We didn't want to start a fire under a lie and give the author any more publicity then he deserved."

Besides, she had already written a book in 2009 about Matt, called *The Meaning of Matthew,* in which she freely discussed her family, warts and all.

"I certainly did not try to whitewash Matt's own issues or ours as a family. So if someone wants to write about that, I have no problem with it. It's the making up stuff that I have a problem with, rehashing those things that are not true and haven't been verified," she said.

What hurt Judy and her family is that people actually believe the lies and misinformation. "But this is how it is," she said. "People who actually believe it are the people who don't believe that there is such thing as a hate crime. They need an explanation of what happened to Matt, other than it was a hate crime. This is what they're going to believe and that's their problem, not mine."

Talking to Judy confirmed what I've always believed. While most people can heal from a loss in their own way and on their own terms, those of us who've been thrust before the media have only two choices: retreat from the public eye or find a way to make our interactions with the media worthy of our loved one's legacy and helpful for the voiceless others. Either decision is understandable, but I believe the latter describes Judy's journey.

The first thing Judy Shepard said to me, at the start of the interview, was how happy she was to participate in this book project. "I think what you are doing is a noble cause," she said. "I think a lot of people who thrive on reading about the pain of others do not realize they are reading about the pain of others."

As our long conversation went on, I knew we hadn't hit the rough side of the mountain yet. I became very interested in how Judy, who was initially intimidated by the media, evolved into a confident advocate who has used the press to help give voice to a community often silenced. And I wondered: What can all of us—survivors, journalists, and the public—learn from her about being sensitive to a family in grief?

To fully understand Judy and Dennis' journey, we have to go back to the day they became an integral part of a national news story.

On Thursday, October 8, 1998, Dennis and Judy were jolted awake when the phone rang at 5 a.m. They were asleep in their home in Saudi Arabia, where Dennis worked as a construction safety manager. They figured it was their twenty-one-year-old son Matt on the other end of the phone. If he had the impulse to talk, Matt, a political science major at the University of Wyoming, would dial them up regardless of the time difference. But the caller wasn't their son; it was an emergency-room doctor from Ivinson Memorial Hospital in Laramie. He had horrible news. Matt had been beaten, and sustained head injuries so serious that he might not make it. The doctor knew nothing else and urged them to catch the next plane to Fort Collins, Colorado, where their son had been transported.

Eighteen hours after leaving Saudi Arabia, Dennis and Judy landed at Minneapolis–St. Paul Airport, where they picked up their youngest son Logan, who was attending a boarding school in the Twin Cities. As the family rushed through the airport to catch a plane to Colorado, Judy caught the quickest glimpse of the *New York Times* and *Minneapolis Star Tribune*; both newspapers had written about her son's attack. She didn't understand why, but it was just one of a series of mystifying occurrences that day.

When they arrived in Colorado, the family had to be sneaked in the back door of the hospital to avoid reporters, who had

surrounded the hospital. But the strangeness of the media attention was quickly forgotten. From the moment they walked into
the hospital room, all their focus was on their oldest son, who was
lying in a coma, his body curled and strapped to wires and tubes,
his head shaved and in bandages.

While Matt fought for his life, the family whispered memories, and talked to him about what they were going to do after
he got out of the hospital. Oblivious that thousands of strangers across the country, and the world, were planning or attending vigils and rallies in Matt's honor, the Shepards focused only
on making Matt comfortable, whether that meant spraying his
favorite cologne in the hospital room or playing his Tracy Chap-
man CDs.

They eventually learned from friends and family who came
to see Matthew that chaos was brewing right outside the hospital
doors. The media were demanding updates, and some were not
playing by the rules; for example, a photographer was caught trying to bypass security officers who had been planted at every door
of the neurosurgery intensive-care unit.

The press had occupied the parking lot and the main lobby,
setting up their own version of a media village. So many emails
came into the hospital that the server crashed, and calls were
coming into the switchboard constantly.

"So, finally, for people we knew—like family and friends who
wanted to check on Matt's condition—we gave them a password,"
Judy said. "For everyone else, the hospital took a message but we
didn't get those messages until much, much later. There were even
movie people and screenwriters calling the hospital."

Thanks to all the work the hospital and police did to hide
the Shepards, the press had no idea what they looked like,
which allowed them to grieve privately for at least a week. "I
guess people nowadays don't even get *that* luxury," Judy told
me. "Nobody was camping out in our front yard, and nobody
was following us home or any of that. They knew our names,

of course, but they didn't know what we looked like until the day of Matt's funeral."

The day of the funeral, thousands of people descended on the small town of Casper, where Judy and Dennis grew up. It was wet and cold outside. Members of the vocal anti-gay group called the Westboro Baptist Church waved their "God Hates Fags" picket signs against the snowy landscape. No one was sure who else the media attention would attract, so police arranged for bomb-sniffing dogs and a SWAT team, and for Dennis, who was to give a statement, to wear a bulletproof vest.

"The reporters were totally obnoxious. The service was held across the street from a private Catholic school, where a cameraman was going into classrooms, while in session, trying to film the procession," Judy said, "And then there were so many people in line trying to get into the church, pretending they were family friends or relatives, that we had to print tickets for people to get into the funeral."

Printing tickets? I wondered how she had the wherewithal to come up with such an idea when she also had to plan and attend her son's funeral.

"I think we just both checked out of anything that was emotional and we moved into this pragmatic, logical, we-need-to-get-things-done mode," she told me. "I said, 'Dennis, these people are telling lies in order to get access. We have to figure out a way to make sure that our family and friends get into the church. . . . Besides that, CNN wanted it on TV and I said, 'Hell no. It's not going on television. That's unkind.' Nowadays, it happens all the time, but I was like 'No, this isn't going to happen.'"

Earlier that day, Judy—after winning an argument with police, who had strongly urged her to stay inside for her own safety—held a white umbrella as she stood beside her husband in front of the Casper City Hall. Satellite trucks, reporters with notebooks, photographers with long-lens cameras, were all she could see. As daunting as the scene was, it would be a defining moment for her, teaching her a lesson she'd never forget.

"It was the first time that the press had ever laid eyes on us," she said. "Dennis made a statement. I did not want to make eye contact with this mass of media. And then as he was reading the statement, I'm thinking, I probably need to make eye contact. I have to do this. I look at them and then I'm thinking this is what they want me to do. I look away."

Caught off guard by her own emotion, Judy started to cry.

"The shutters just go crazy," she said. "In this moment, I'm thinking, 'This is why they are here—just to see this broken family cry and shed tears.' That media saying, 'If it bleeds it leads,' became very clear to me, as well as how fluidly the media works."

From then on, Judy learned to stay in control of her emotions and to never veer away from information she wanted to relay: First, discuss the violence and how it affected her family. Second, describe what it was like to lose a son in the way that she did. "The press needs to know that this is hard and the attack was ridiculous and stupid and cruel and it should never happen again," she said. "And the only way we are going to stop it is if we pay attention."

I told Judy that sometimes the only way to get the public's attention is to be graphic. I thought of the horrified looks on people's faces when I recount every wound that my brother and Nicole endured. I use very violent language when I speak in public. It took me a long time to be comfortable with doing that, but my brother was viciously stabbed to death and Nicole nearly decapitated—so when you hear those words it's like, *Wow, holy shit*. I believe it reminds people of the brutality and the senseless-ness and hate attached to a crime. It sensitizes people to death, and tragedy—occurrences so common nowadays that we have all grown accustomed to hearing about them. I wondered how

Judy felt about the media being graphic when retelling what happened to her son.

"Do you know the story about Emmett Till's mom?" she asked me.

Emmett Till was an African-American teenager killed in Mississippi by two white men. The teen, who was from Chicago, was visiting relatives that summer when he allegedly made a pass at a white woman while buying bubble gum at the local store. Several days later, after two men kidnapped him from his great-uncle's house, Emmett's body was found at the edge of Talla-hatchie River. A fan used for ginning cotton was tied to his neck; an eye had been gouged out, and he was shot in the head. After the body was discovered and returned to Chicago, his mother insisted on a public funeral service with an open casket to show the world what had been done to her baby boy.

"That's exactly how we thought about it," Judy said. "We even had that discussion before we knew about Emmett Till. We thought maybe we should have shown the world what he really looked like after the attack so that they would see for themselves what happened. You want people to understand the senselessness and how absolutely cruel and ridiculous and absurd the whole situation is. But we knew what Matt's wishes were. He wanted to be cremated."

Judy and I talked a lot about her frustration with the media, but I was curious: Did the journalists ever get it right?

"There's very few times that they ever got it right. Even the interviews I do now, I don't read because I know there's going to be something that's going to be wrong. In fact, we got a request from a woman writing a chapter in a textbook. She had every single fact wrong about Matt, every single one—in a textbook! What happens is, very few people do their own original research. They use someone else's article and that person's mistakes get perpetuated over and over and over.

"I get the idea that the true journalists think they are going to write an unbiased article. Well, that's a fallacy. Everyone brings their own bias, from the words that they choose to use to the way they string the words together, and every journalist will create their own picture. We all have bias, all of us do, and they may think they are being totally unbiased but they never are."

Despite all of her hesitations, I wondered, why did she finally give in and sit down with the media?

"We understood that because of the volume of the media requests we were getting, we were going to have to go ahead and talk to them eventually. We just didn't respond to any requests until a month later."

After the funeral, Dennis went back to Saudi and Judy stayed in Wyoming to manage some loose ends before returning home.

"We sort of escaped and nobody knew how to get in touch with us. There were a couple of phone calls on our phone in Saudi from the media," she said. "I don't know how they got our number there, but we just really didn't respond to any of them. Ultimately, we chose the first interview to be with Katie Couric because we felt that she would never ask a stupid question like 'How does it feel?' because she had just lost her husband."

Listening to her story, I could see the growth Judy experienced since Matt's death. She was forced to evolve, and do so quickly, like it or not. After sixteen years, she's learned to be selective and disciplined in the way she uses the media to help further the LGBT agenda.

"Legally, the gay community now is approaching equality. Back then it was just a hope and a dream. But what's happening now that things are good is that the haters will hate all the more, and they will commit more hate crimes against the gay community. They are more vocal and more demonstrative," she said. "And people who support the gay community have gone one of two ways: they have become silent because they don't want to attract attention to themselves or they have become more vocal and outspoken. So there is still that really ugly underbelly that has gotten just uglier and in some ways bigger, but the voice supporting has also gotten louder and bigger too."

Only a few families ever have to face worldwide media the way Judy and Dennis did, but surviving families today still have to face a constant barrage of stories, tweets, Facebook comments, and a twenty-four-hour news cycle. In the aftermath of their son's murder, Judy and Dennis emerged as brave souls and strong parents; I wondered if Judy had advice for other families forced to heal in the spotlight.

"You don't owe the media anything," she said. "Don't talk to them unless you want to. Don't let them pressure you into doing it, just because they need the story. It's their issue, not yours. Unless you're ready to talk about it, don't do it, because that message that you end up sending may not be the one that you want the world to see."

Judy actually told me she never thought that sixteen years later, she'd still be talking about her son's death to the public.

"We thought in a couple years, Matt's story would just be another story."

She was wrong. The truth is, his story, like so many other high profile cases, will never cease to exist. With the birth of the internet and cable news, stories from twenty, thirty, forty years ago are regurgitated, reported, investigated, and told over and over again as if the violence just happened. Just Google "victims" and "anniversary" together and you will see the countless headlines reminding us of or even introducing us to, American tragedies: "Fort Hood Victim's Kin Holding Memorials," "On 10th 9/11 Anniversary, Wounds Fresh as Healing Continues," "On a Day It Can Never Escape, Dallas Tries to Heal" (marking the fiftieth anniversary of President John F. Kennedy's assassination). Every time those anniversary stories pop up, moms, dads, daughters, and sons are forced to relive those tragedies. Looking back allows people to remember, reflect, and respect, but too often these "anniversaries" of public tragedies are emotional pornography substituting for real journalism.

Judy and I both agreed there is not much we can do to stop those stories from running, and we also agreed that survivors like us never reference a death of a loved one as an anniversary, as if we are celebrating something. But Judy was willing to ignore the insensitivity if it meant publicity for the work she does to help suppress homophobia.

"We milk the anniversaries for what they're worth and totally bring money into the foundation to continue the work," she said. "We put all feelings about the media calling these deaths anniversaries, and that the interviews are in bad taste, aside, and take advantage to talk about what we want to talk about. We even let them call it an anniversary if they want to. We make it clear we don't call it that, but if they want to they can."

The goal on those dates, she explained, is to remind people what happened and to encourage them to help the foundation with their work or send donations.

"Some things require mercenary steps," Judy said.

Here's another woman, like Debra Tate, and like others in this book, who learned to use the media for good.

I wanted to know when that shift actually happened. Judy said she began to get smarter about a year after she cried in front of the media on the day of her son's funeral.

"I had the a-ha moment. I thought, 'I can offer myself and my services to every national organization to raise the profile of the situation facing the LGBT community in today's world.' And that is exactly what I did. I did a press conference for one of several organizations in 1999. I began reading a statement about the importance of the hate-crime bill and I started to cry. The media went just wacky yet again," she said.

That was the moment Judy thought, "If they're going to do this to me, then I'm going to do this to them." She decided that every time reporters called for an interview, she'd find a way to talk about the foundation.

"I will just always work it in somehow," she said. "It was like, if you're going to use me to sell papers, then I'm going to go ahead and use you to grow the movement and educate the public."

MARIE MONVILLE

Wife of the Amish Shooter

October 2, 2006

Top: Marie and Dan Monville, married May 2007 (courtesy of Carli Bowman Photography). *Bottom:* Marie and Amish Shooter Charlie Roberts on their wedding day, November 1996.

B efore any of it happened, Marie Monville lived an unremarkable and sheltered life.

"I was a stay-at-home mom. I loved being a wife. I loved being a mom. Those were my two lifelong dreams from the time I was a little girl," Marie told me. "I was a great student in high school and all my teachers assumed I would go to college, and they were quite disappointed when I said that I was not going, but that I was planning to get married and have kids and that's all I wanted. I was very private, reserved. I had never been one to be center stage. I wouldn't have wanted to be in the spotlight. But everything that I knew to be true about life changed that day."

That day was October 2, 2006, when Marie's husband, Charles Carl Roberts, stormed into a one-room Amish schoolhouse in an idyllic village in Lancaster County, Pennsylvania, and opened fire on ten Amish girls, murdering five of them before turning the gun on himself. The tragedy shocked the nation, not just because it was a brutal killing of innocent girls, but also because it happened in Amish country, a traditionalist Christian community known for its simplicity and tradition of nonviolence.

I remember seeing the ongoing broadcast of the teary-eyed Amish families in their bonnets and big hats, trying to avoid the cameras. I was curious about these people, whose quiet lives had been so suddenly interrupted by tragedy; their world felt so mysterious and private. And of course, I wondered about the shooter—and his wife. What could she tell us about him? I wasn't alone. The world had fixed its sights on the twenty-eight-year-old milkman's daughter and mom of three, named Marie Roberts at the time, to answer as to how this could have happened.

"Every facet of my life changed, from that very place of being so quiet and reserved, to having no way to protect that anymore because now the world is looking in," Marie said.

Feeling like a woman on the run, she avoided the media whenever possible, refusing their calls, taking side streets when reporters were around. She hid at the homes of relatives and was shielded by the Amish community itself when the media pulled out their cameras.

But she couldn't dodge the public's judgment. Questions about how much she knew about her husband's plans still came, sometimes out of the mouths of strangers, and sometimes even written on the faces of people she knew. They even rolled over in her own head. Had there been any clues? What had set him off? What hadn't she seen?

What she couldn't understand was why everyone wanted to talk to *her*. Not only did she live an uneventful life, she told me, she did not have the answers they were all looking for.

"I said, 'Okay God, I trust I'm never going to have this concrete explanation for any of this,'" Marie recalled, "'but I am going to trust that you will do something even in the midst of this that I can't see, that you're going to bring beauty from ashes.'"

Marie's tale, I began to realize as we talked, was not about a milkman's daughter becoming the shooter's wife (a label the media gave her); it was about a shy and deeply religious woman who clung to her faith, and eventually found joy and enough strength to step out of the shadows to tell her own story. I was fascinated by her powerful journey from grief to grace.

"It really was that complete transformation on so many levels," she said. "I had to move forward, though I didn't really have a choice in that. Working through it, I discovered wonderful things about myself that I probably wouldn't have ever thought existed. But in the moment, even that didn't make it any easier."

October 2, 2006, was a very clear, crisp day. It was an Indian summer, she recalled. The fall leaves were starting to change but it was still warm and beautiful.

At about 8:30 that morning, Charlie and Marie walked their oldest children, Abigail, 7, and Bryce, 5, to the bus stop. Charlie kissed them goodbye, and went off to work in Marie's grandfather's blue truck.

The day was like every other day. The clip-clop of horses' hooves, the girls in bonnets, and the men donning wide-brimmed hats and long beards were all normal sights and sounds to Marie, who grew up living next door to and among more Amish neighbors than not, though she isn't Amish herself.

"My great-grandparents had started a milk transportation business. They picked up milk at the Amish farms and delivered it to the dairy. So I had been on a lot of the Amish farms, riding along in the truck with my dad and grandfather as a little girl, and then Charlie started to drive a tractor-trailer after we had been married for a couple of years. He was very familiar with a lot of those families as well."

While Charlie was supposedly hauling milk that day, Marie was home with their eighteen-month-old son, Carson.

She had just poured herself a cup of coffee when the phone rang at 11 a.m. When she answered, the most chilling, flat voice—her husband's—told her he wasn't coming home.

"That's when I knew something was going on, but he didn't say what was happening."

His conversation, though difficult to follow, was one she'll never forget.

"I was very much concerned that he was going to take his own life, but I did not know, at that point, that it would involve anyone else. And so I was just begging him on the phone not to do whatever he was planning to do and saying to him there has to be another way, there is always another way.

"He wasn't answering me and before we hung up the phone he said he had left a letter for me on our dresser. He told me where to find it. He said to tell his family and tell my family that he loved them and he hung up the phone. I went and found the letter he left for me and read it. I had never read a suicide note before, but I knew that this must be one. I immediately called 911. I could tell by the questions the dispatcher was asking me that he already knew a lot more than I did. It was about that time that I started to hear a lot of sirens going—there were helicopters flying up ahead and police cars racing up the street. In the pit of my stomach, as much as I wanted to deny it, I knew that this was not a coincidence—that it all had to be tied together."

After she hung up from the 911 operator, she called her mother to come over right away. Meanwhile, the haunting sounds of sirens grew louder. It wasn't an unfamiliar sound; Marie could picture the Amish volunteer firemen racing to Bart Fire Hall by foot-powered scooters, while everyone else, "the English," arrived in cars and trucks. But after Charlie's phone call, the sound felt like a confirmation that something was terribly wrong.

Her fears were soon realized. From the window, Marie watched as three cars pulled into her yard; one was a police car, the other two were unmarked. She wanted to run to the door, to ask what they knew, but her feet wouldn't move. Then the knock came.

"I said, 'It's Charlie, isn't it?' and they said, 'Yes.' I said, 'He's dead, isn't he?' They said, 'Yes.'"

She sat on the couch as several uniformed officers and detectives started to ask her questions and answered hers. "It was very easy for them to see that I had no information at all, and so it became this process of them telling me what happened."

They told her that around 10:30 a.m., Charlie had ordered the Amish boys, a teacher, and a teacher's aide to leave the schoolhouse, then barricaded the doors, rounded up the ten girls, ages seven to twelve, against the blackboard, and tied them up before shooting them.

The story the detectives told seemed implausible. How could this be true? But she could tell by the somber look on their faces that they had witnessed the bloody aftermaths themselves.

She felt her mind spiraling, but had a vision of God lifting a flower before it could touch the ground; that image kept her from falling deeper into shock and despair. She mourned for the Amish families; she knew them well, had grown up waving to and chatting with them. And they all knew and adored Charlie, who picked up their milk and brought it to the dairies.

As she sat there listening to the officers, she had to come to terms with the fact that she was suddenly a widow. What was she going to tell her children? As she grappled with these thoughts, the detectives pressed her for more information, asking deeply personal questions about her husband's mental state.

Still in shock, she assured them that Charlie was a kind, quiet man who, while withdrawn at times, showed no signs that he was hiding such hate and rage. But Marie showed them the suicide letter, in which Charlie expressed how angry he was at God and himself over the death of Elise, their first child, who died in their arms twenty minutes after being born nearly ten years earlier in 1997.

I wondered aloud if she thought this was a psychotic break, or something else. What she described to me were bouts of depression her husband had struggled with over the death of their daughter, but nothing that would indicate he might one day turn violent.

"He would go through these periods of being withdrawn, and it wasn't like every three weeks he would feel this way—it was several times a year that he would become withdrawn and I knew that it had to do with the loss of our first daughter. I would ask him 'How are you feeling?' and 'What's bothering you?' and those kinds of things, but he never wanted to talk about it. We had been with family in the days before all of this happened, spending some time together, having dinner together, grilling outside; it was fun. No one saw anything that you could put your finger on and say 'that's exactly why this happened.' I realize it wasn't just me who missed the signs, but how could we have been with my family and his family and no one noticed anything off? How could we all have missed this?"

I knew it must have been hard for Marie to reconcile how things ended. Time and again, people asked her these same questions, about whether there was something she missed. Strangers asked her if she could sleep at night, knowing that she had lived with a mass murderer.

But I wonder, is it right to ask a wife to speculate about secrets buried deep in her husband's heart or theorize about the twisted logic of a man who had privately descended into madness? It would seem to be an impossible task.

As Marie sat in her home that day, talking to detectives, grappling with the enormity of what they were telling her, struggling with the shame, the pain and horror, she also faced another problem: the national media were about to invade the village, and they were all going to want to talk to her.

"How long do I have before the media arrives?" Marie asked one of the policemen. The officer was surprised the press hadn't already descended on her doorstep, but Marie later learned that because the small, remote village they lived in was not actually on the map, it confused the press and gave Marie—along with her father, who had joined her—just enough time to rush through packing clothes and other necessities before heading to her parents' home to find respite.

"Our pastor was our spokesperson and I wrote a statement that he read to the media: 'The man who did this today is not the Charlie that I've been married to for almost ten years. My husband is loving, supportive, thoughtful, all the things you'd always want and more.'"

It wasn't long before the media discovered Marie was hiding at her parents' residence. Photographers with telescopic lenses were caught in a neighbor's yard. Marie's brother, Ken, noticed a photographer lurking in their parents' bushes.

"The reporters left message after message or they tried to get ahold of other people to talk to me," Marie said. "There were some reporters who were respectful of me, and of the fact that I had no interest in talking, and there were others who were not."

Ken, who Marie describes as an imposing fellow with a shaved head, stood at their parents' door, telling any reporter who'd dare walk toward him that Marie didn't want to talk and they shouldn't call again. But many continued to call, and the family would eventually flee to Marie's aunt's home to hide out.

"At one point, one of the police detectives called a reporter back for me and said, 'Do not call her again.'"

Marie was heartbroken that the photographers were taking pictures of the grieving Amish, disrespecting their belief that photographs violate biblical commandments and that posing for them is a sign of pride, and a stark contrast to the Amish tenet of humility.

Despite their own grief and mourning, six Amish men walked down the street to visit her parents' home. Marie was shocked, and called for her father, who met them in the driveway. Marie could see from the window, the men embracing her father's slumped shoulders. He would later tell her the reason for their visit: they had not only forgiven Charlie, but were deeply worried about her.

The kindness the men showed toward her family warmed her soul, but the invasion of the media was causing Marie anxiety.

She'd later receive word that back at her house, the media had set up camp. Without reporters seeing, she sneaked back to her home and put a No Trespassing sign up in her yard.

When Marie finally returned to her home, a week after the tragedy, she realized it wasn't just the media encroaching on her privacy: One morning, a stranger came to her door. The woman said, "I just have to meet you and see for myself, because I don't believe what everybody saying, that you didn't know."

Around the same time, a florist came to her door with a large bouquet of flowers.

Marie recalled, "The florist was like, 'You're never going to believe who these are from' and I said, 'Try me,' because I had heard from just about everybody by that point."

It wasn't even five minutes after Marie walked back into the home with the flowers, reading the card from the sender, that a producer from a big news show called: "Hey, did you get the flowers? We were wondering if you wanted to come on our show and do an interview."

Marie knew they hadn't sent the flowers because they cared about her or her family, but rather, in Marie's words, it was "an opportunity to open the door and start some kind of discussion."

But support would eventually come, and from all over. Letters sent to her filled entire crates. "People from across the world were sending us notes, telling us that they were praying for us, just encouraging me."

The Amish were the most supportive of all. They showered her with gifts, food, and compassion. Dozens of Amish men and women, including the parents of the five dead girls, attended Charlie's funeral. "One of their fundamental principles is that whole emphasis on forgiveness," Marie explained to me. "So to them, that was a very automatic thing. It's not to say that it wasn't difficult, but that's still a part of who they are."

On the day of Charlie's burial, reporters with their television trucks and high-powered lenses stood outside the cemetery in full force to capture the family grieving.

Marie was devastated and felt caged. All the work she had put into keeping her family from the media's gaze was unraveling right before her eyes.

But what happened next was extraordinary: Like angels in black, the Amish appeared, dozens of them, coming to her rescue. With their capes blowing in the wind, they turned their backs on the cameras, forming a semi-circle, allowing for a small opening in order for the cars packed with her family to pull into the cemetery. Then they closed the circle to hide Marie and her family from the media's view.

"The way it played out was remarkable," Marie said. Their kind gesture gave her hope that things were going to be okay.

I asked her, when did the healing start? Her answer was unexpected.

It started, she said, minutes after Charlie's cryptic phone call.

Calling it her "walk-on-water moment," referring to how Jesus tested his disciples' faith by challenging them to follow him across the Sea of Galilee, she found herself looking up to the ceiling and praying. "I felt such an overwhelming sense of God being with me and of his peace being over me, just something that I had not previously experienced to that depth. The things I experienced that day were very powerful, and I knew that he was doing something that I couldn't see and that he was already working things that I was unaware of. That's not to say that I didn't feel pain and sorrow and a whole range of emotions. It's been a gradual process."

I respect the way Marie has processed the traumatic event that plagued her life, and the way she has evolved because of it. But her journey toward healing is very different than the one I am on: It's no secret I choose not to forgive the person who I believe killed my brother. But the Amish immediately forgave Charlie for his heinous acts, though I imagine they fiercely struggle with it still, and their decision to do so inspired a nation.

There's another big difference in the way Marie and I processed what happened to us—our religious beliefs.

To me, Marie's faith in God and the church is the most beautiful part of her story, because it helped her to heal. I shared with Marie a vivid memory of my father, as we sat at Ron's gravesite many years ago. My father was much more religious than I, but after Ron was killed, he began to question God. He'd say things like, "How could my God do this to me? I've been a devout Jew my whole life. I did everything he told me. I prayed, I followed the rules, I've gone to temple. I had faith."

I felt such sadness for him, because he was struggling with not just the loss of his only son, but also with his faith in God. I remember apologizing to him after what I said next: "Thank goodness I didn't have to cope with *that*, too."

Marie understood. However, she said she felt *grateful* because her tragedy brought her closer to God rather than drive her away.

But healing is not a straightforward process; it's full of ups and downs. "Sometimes out of the blue for no apparent reason you can be reminded of something that kind of takes you back to the trauma. But right now, I think for me and my family, we are at a great place. We are continuing to understand new things about ourselves and see the beauty of who we are."

Four months after the tragedy, Marie relied on her faith yet again when she did the unexpected: she became engaged to Dan Monville, an insurance agent and a family acquaintance.

"Not everyone was happy about it," she said. "Even the newspaper wrote a story about it, with the headline 'Mass Killer's Widow Plans to Remarry.'"

Marie understood their reservations. She, too, worried it was too early to marry, but ultimately she trusted in the incredible bond she and Dan had formed after the shooting. Love blossomed; it all just clicked. Marie said God assured her that Dan was the right man for her and her children.

"I think it was difficult for people to imagine that I could be in a healthy place. So there was criticism, almost a rising up against

Dan and I, and we were very much aware that would happen. We tried to give them grace, thinking, 'Well they don't really know what God has been doing in our hearts.' I remember thinking, 'Gosh we have just been through this horrendous season of our lives, if there is a glimmer of hope of something beautiful, why wouldn't you want that for our family, why wouldn't you want that for us?'"

They bought a home ten miles from her old home, blended their families, and married in 2007.

Her family isn't just surviving what Charlie did, they're thriving. The oldest of Marie and Dan's five children, Marie's stepdaughter, is now out of college and on her own. "We have two in high school, one in junior high and one in elementary school."

When Dan and Marie are not busy with their roles as parents, helping with homework and driving the children to extracurricular activities, Marie speaks to churches and community organizations.

How did she transform from someone who avoided the media whenever possible to someone who voluntarily spoke about her experiences? Reporters, church groups, and strangers never stopped wanting to hear from her, and in 2011, five years after the tragedy, the news requests flooded in. But instead of immediately declining, she considered speaking. She could feel a shift was happening.

She eventually submitted a personal statement to the local newspaper. That was her first step.

From the response she received, she realized people were not being nosey or judgmental; they just wanted to hear how she overcame.

She stopped running and began to accept what happened to her as part of her life, even, in some ways, accepting the "Amish Shooter's Wife" label. Doing so would later help her find the courage to tell her own story of finding joy over adversity.

Slowly she began to say yes to invitations to speak at churches and community organizations. When large groups of her Amish neighbors showed up to support her, she knew she had found her voice.

"Someone once said to me that when your pain becomes your platform, there's something really beautiful that happens with that. And it's so true that when you can allow the things that have happened to you to not necessarily define you but somehow become a good part of someone else's journey, it just takes the story in a completely different direction."

When you experience a tragedy, others who are struggling in their own lives often feel a kinship with you. "They trust you with the hard things that they have gone through, in hopes you can encourage them," Marie said.

She's maintained relationships with the families of the girls her husband killed. "It's not that we see them all the time, but it's not unusual to run into them at Costco or to get together, maybe one-on-one in their homes, and sit around and chat together."

Her family has something else to celebrate. They are also in the process of adopting a child from South Africa. "It's pretty exciting as well. We don't know yet whether it will be a boy or a girl or what their age will be, we just know that it will be a child that's older than five."

In 2013, Marie wrote a book, *One Light Still Shines*, about how she overcame tragedy and found happiness, but doing so meant she had to face one of her biggest fears.

"I knew I would have to talk to reporters, and that I wouldn't be able to shy away from them this time. I think my perspective on talking to the media really shifted knowing that I hadn't said anything for all those years and really the ball was in my court now.

"I could give them any answer that I chose. I didn't have that pressure or feeling like, 'Oh my goodness what are they going to ask me?' or 'What am I going to say?'" she said. "All the things that I kind of felt about those fears initially changed; I could stay true to the message and what I wanted to share, and I realized that whatever I said was up to me."

DAVE AND MARY NEESE

Parents of teen murder victim Skylar Neese

July 6, 2012

Top: Dave, Mary, and Skylar, 2003, when Skylar was in second grade.
Bottom left: Skylar, 2012, at age sixteen, with her dog Lilu. *Bottom right:*
From left to right: Shelia Eddy, Rachel Shoaf, and Skylar, 2012.

Mary and Dave's only child, Skylar Neese, was a typical American sixteen-year-old girl: she worked at Wendy's, made good grades, and loved being on Facebook or Twitter.

The Neeses are hard workers—Dave, a big teddy bear of a man, is a product assembler at Walmart, and Mary, a sweet-faced woman with a dimple in one cheek, is an administrative assistant in a cardiac lab.

Still, money was tight for them in their hometown of Star City, West Virginia. So Skylar kept a straight-A average at University High School because she knew she'd need a scholarship for college in order to earn a law degree one day.

But as hard as she worked, the auburn-haired, blue-eyed beauty played just as hard.

When she wasn't studying or working, she spent every waking hour, it seemed, with her two closest friends: Rachel Shoaf, a beautiful redheaded honor student and the star of University High's school plays, and Shelia Eddy, a drop-dead gorgeous brunette and fellow honor student, who was the wildest of the group and had been Skylar's best friend since they were eight.

Like most teens these days, the trio spent their free time tweeting and retweeting and posting selfies. And they were just as inseparable at school as they were online.

But at some point the bond between them began to break, and Skylar became the odd man out. In a string of Twitter comments, Skylar revealed what seemed to be anger with her best friends.

On May 31, 2012, Skylar tweeted, *you're a two-faced bitch, and obviously fucking stupid if you didn't think I was going to find out.*

On July 4, she wrote, *sick of being in the fucking home, thanks "friends," love hanging out with you too.*

By this point, Rachel and Shelia had already decided to put into action their long-plotted plan to kill Skylar.

On July 5, 2012, the two girls, pretending to make up with Skylar, invited her to come with them on a late-night joyride like old times.

Skylar hadn't completely forgiven them in full, as her retweet at 11:15 p.m. of another Twitter user's tweet seems to suggest: *All I do is hope.* Still, at 12:31 a.m. on July 6, she sneaked out of her bedroom room window to Shelia's awaiting silver Toyota.

As Shelia later told detectives, the three girls drove to a wooded area across the West Virginia border to Pennsylvania, roughly thirty miles from Skylar's home; it was a familiar spot, where the three of them would occasionally go to smoke marijuana.

They drove down the long dirt road, Skylar quiet in the back and the other girls chatty in front, both of them hiding kitchen knives under their clothes. Packed in the trunk was a shovel Rachel stole from her father's house, paper towels, bleach, two changes of clean clothes, and Handi Wipes.

The girls got out to smoke, but couldn't get the lighter to work. When Skylar turned her back to get her lighter from the car, Rachel counted to three, and the two girls began stabbing her.

Shelia, Skylar's best friend in the world, the person she once wrote in a diary that she "couldn't live without," stabbed Skylar fifty times. Skylar fought back, but eventually all she could do was ask, "Why?"

After Rachel and Shelia watched her take her last breath, they dragged her to the side of the road, near a creek. They tried to dig a hole to bury her body, but the ground was too hard, so they just covered her with branches and dirt. The two girls then returned to their car, stripped naked, cleaned up with the wipes, and stashed their bloody clothes in a garbage bag. The entire ordeal took about three hours.

When Skylar didn't show up at her job that day, Dave called 911. In the recording, Dave sounds torn up. "I have a sixteen-year-old daughter. She hasn't been home . . . I'm scared to death."

Dave told me he just knew she wouldn't stay out all night like that. And she wouldn't just leave home. "She loved her mom and dad to death and told us that every single day."

The final image of Skylar, getting into an unknown car after midnight, was captured on the grainy black-and-white surveillance video at the apartment complex where the Neeses lived. The image confirmed to the parents that something was wrong, but to police it only confirmed that she had probably run away.

Mary immediately began canvassing the neighborhood, putting up flyers, and calling Skylar's friends. Several weeks later, Mary and Dave would establish a closed Facebook group called TEAMSKYLAR2012, to provide support for friends and family and offer updates on the search.

When it came to reporting on Skylar's disappearance, social media dominated from the very beginning, scooping the traditional media outlets, which did not pick up the story until three or four days after Skylar's disappearance.

Those first few days after Mary and Dave reported Skylar missing, family, friends, high-school students, and armchair detectives on the internet all passed along pertinent information and prayers online. They followed trails and clues, and eventually they'd expose the pretty little killers with such a vengeance that the world would take notice.

The fascination with the case was obvious in the voice of the anchor on a *Dateline* episode about Skylar's murder. "Tonight we're going to take you into a secret world that's going to stun you. Teenagers. Social media. And murder."

Both Dave and Mary were featured prominently on the episode, but talking to media isn't Mary's cup of tea. She preferred handling the close communication with people on Facebook, while Dave reluctantly became the family spokesperson for newspapers and television stations.

"Mary wasn't used to the publicity and nor was I, but I handled that part a little bit better and she did her own thing better than I did," Dave said.

Mary found the traditional media's mere presence intrusive. "I didn't like it from the beginning. I hid. That's why they always talked to Dave. I didn't want the attention. I didn't want any part of being in front of the media. I didn't do radio, TV, or newspaper. I'm a private person. I did the background stuff, I worked on the computer, I did Facebook, did flyers, that whole thing."

In the meantime, Shelia and Rachel were putting on the best acts of their lives. Both attended a candlelight vigil for Skylar. Shelia who was like a second daughter to Mary and Dave, even went with Mary to search the area for Skylar. At one point, she even asked Mary if she could sit in Skylar's bedroom. Mary and Dave supported the girls, even as people on Facebook and Twitter were outright accusing them of killing Skylar.

"I felt so bad for them," Mary said. "Every time Shelia would come over to see me she would be crying and I thought she was crying because she missed Skylar. Yeah, little did I know; we were fools. We felt so stupid."

But some of the people who followed the case on social media—classmates of the girls at University High, friends and family in discussion groups, and even strangers who closely followed crimes—were not fooled by the killers, not for a second.

In retrospect, these online detectives did a lot of work for police, dissecting previous exchanges the three girls made on Twitter and urging the girls to tell police and the family what they knew.

At times, they'd just say it like they saw it—calling Shelia and Rachel killers and ripping them apart for not turning themselves in.

To Dave, who was one of Shelia and Rachel's biggest defenders, it was a sickening thing to witness, this virtual beatdown.

He felt for Shelia when she posted a Facebook message on August 10: *all I want for my best friend to come home. I wish I knew something to give the police a lead or so she can come home but I don't know ANYTHING . . . I wish I knew something like everybody thinks I do. come home skylar, its been five weeks too long. I miss and love you.*

Dave typed: *Love you Shelia I want her back too.*

Shelia wrote back: *love you too Dave.*

"When local police, the FBI, and state police started questioning the girls at school," Dave said, "I told them to 'leave these girls alone, they're fine, they make good grades, they're good kids, they don't do anything wrong, leave 'em alone.' They were Skylar's best friends, I mean, my God, they wouldn't have anything to do with her disappearance."

People on social media were initially kind to Dave and Mary, even as rumors swirled on the internet that painted Skylar in a less than flattering light. And as time went on, those rumors continued to intensify. "Some of the things that people were coming up with—like Skylar was a heroin addict hiding out on skid row, she didn't want to come home because we were mean, and all this other crap—was just stupid," Dave explained.

Soon, the internet turned from a portal of good intentions into a virtual pit of lies.

One critic was a distant relative who Dave didn't even know.

"At one point a cousin of mine said that I had raped Skylar, got her pregnant, and she was hiding in a halfway house in Pennsylvania, and Mary knew where she was but she was keeping her away from me," Dave said. "We told the police we would take lie-detector tests, but the police never once asked us to. They believed us wholeheartedly."

The ugly lies about Mary and Dave doubled the pain of not knowing whether Skylar was alive or dead. They both tried their best to answer as many questions on Facebook as possible, while trying to ignore negative posts, which was always difficult.

"I would read stuff and I was furious," David said. "I wanted to go out and find the people who wrote it and knock 'em in the head because it was just totally preposterous. I said, 'How could you do this? My daughter is missing, how could you make assumptions that I would ever hurt her, or that I did this or that I did that?'"

One of the officers that Mary and Dave talked to the most gave Dave sound advice. "He said, 'Dave, don't read it.' And I'd say, 'But it's out there and other people are reading it,' and he'd say, 'So? Just don't read it.' So that's how I got through some of it, but I was furious about some of that stuff."

Thankfully, the mainstream media never did publish the lies. Nor did they print the names of Rachel and Shelia, both minors, despite the fact everyone knew police had their eyes on them.

In traditional journalism, there is an ethical standard that most reporters follow, which helps prevent reporting mistruths. It doesn't prevent this every time, but it's a system that has been honed over many years of practice. When journalists lose sight of that standard, the damage can be significant.

While plenty of citizen journalists on the internet do good work—and in cases like Skylar's they even see things the traditional media doesn't—everyday people, without journalism training but armed with a Twitter, Instagram, or Facebook account, can cause an overwhelming amount of pain.

In the Neeses' case, the mainstream media was much kinder than the online community. Maybe their extreme good behavior was the only way they could compete with social media. By getting into David's good graces, they landed interviews with him that prevented major news agencies from getting scooped by amateurs.

"The traditional news people would tell us how sorry they were, and how much they thought Skylar was so beautiful. For the most part they didn't bother us a lot. People showing up at our house and sitting outside our door, that only happened a couple of times," Dave said.

It was actually the people who followed the story on Twitter and Facebook, he said, who intensified their grief. What began as a safe place online to serve as an information feeder for friends, family, and even for police became a forum for unsubstantiated rumors. Looking back, the social media activity surrounding Skylar's disappearance is a cautionary tale of how the reckless behavior on the internet of repeating stories without fact-checking can be incredibly hurtful to those on the receiving end. It also shows us the sheer power of social media—of rattling off information in 140 characters or less—and the insurmountable impact that can have, good or bad.

Nearly seven months after Skylar went missing, her family received excruciating confirmation of their worst fears: Skylar was dead.

But police kept one important piece of information from them: Rachel had confessed.

A few weeks earlier Rachel's mother called 911. "I have a sixteen-year-old teen," she told the operator. "She's hitting us. She's screaming at us. She running through the neighborhood—" And then, to someone screaming in the background, "No, no, no . . . this ends here." The exasperated mother finally says, "Please hurry!"

Police rushed in and handcuffed a kicking-and-screaming Rachel before putting her in the back of the police car. Eventually admitted to a psychiatric institution, Rachel left less than a week later, on January 3, 2013. That day, she went straight to her attorney's office and confessed to police that she helped Shelia kill Skylar. She led police to the Appalachian backwoods, near where Skylar was killed, but she couldn't find the exact spot where they had left their friend's body. Returning to the woods on their own, police eventually found Skylar's decomposing body on January 16, though her skull was nowhere to be found.

Someone on social media, not a reporter from the traditional press, was the first to comment on the discovery. At 11:53 a.m., a

Twitter user with the pseudonym "JosieSnyder," a phantom poster (who some people believe was really a police officer, and who was known to taunt and pressure the girls on Twitter), sent out a subtle but mournful tweet: *the SKY is so gloomy today:(*

"Whoever they were, Josie Snyders' sources were solid," wrote Daleen Berry and Geoffrey C. Fuller, authors of *Pretty Little Killers*. "Her tweet about Skylar being found came on the morning of the same day she was found."

Finding the body wasn't the end of Dave and Mary's trauma. Six months after Skylar was found, after a bitter battle with the local coroner, the couple finally got access to their daughter's remains, including her skull, which police later discovered in the wooded area.

I asked Mary how she felt about people knowing the grisly details of her daughter's murder; did it feel like an invasion of privacy?

"We want people to know the terror she suffered," Mary said, as she began to describe the brutal torture her only daughter endured. "People don't understand the real true horror that went with this. The public should know that on the count of three they started stabbing her; that Skylar had been stabbed again and again and again, and that Skylar tried to run and they tackled her down and they just stood over her until her last breath and waited until she stopped making noises. She did the gurgling and all that and they just stood over her and listened until it stopped, and people should know they made sure she was dead before they left."

To Mary and Dave, not telling what truly happened to their daughter is like describing Shelia and Rachel *just* as sixteen-year-old girls rather than cold-blooded killers. It paints a whole new picture.

It might sound like a contradiction when a survivor complains that they want the media to be less invasive, and then, in the next breath, say it's okay to reveal graphic details of their loved one's murder, but it's not. Rather, it underscores how emotionally removed the media is from what the family actually wants or needs.

"I think the graphic details reinforce the fact that Shelia and Rachel do need to remain in prison, they do not need to get out on parole. It makes people realize how horribly brutal they were to her," Mary said.

The law agreed with her.

In May 2013, Rachel Shoaf was sentenced to thirty years imprisonment following her guilty plea of second-degree murder; she is eligible for parole after ten years. In September of that year, West Virgina's prosecuting attorney named Shelia the second killer; she was charged with kidnapping, first-degree murder, and conspiracy to commit murder. She pleaded not guilty at the time of her arraignment, but four days prior to her case going to trial in January 2014 changed her plea to guilty and was sentenced to life. She is eligible for parole after fifteen years.

Even though both girls pleaded guilty to murder, it's still not exactly clear *why* they killed Skylar.

Rachel told authorities, "We just didn't like her anymore." But others, including police, believe the two girls were worried Skylar would disclose their lesbian relationship.

Now that everyone knows what really happened to Skylar, Dave told me people in the public continue to send their condolences and support them.

"The ones that were positive always stood behind us," Dave told me. "Most of them are saying how sorry they still are, and that they are going to write letters to the parole board to keep these girls in jail, and they still tell us how beautiful Skylar was."

Dave said the location where Skylar was murdered has been turned into a makeshift memorial for her.

"People can stop there and sit, because we have a bench there, and they can put flowers there or whatever they want. Some put little trinkets; she loved candy, so they put all kinds of candy out there. It's just a little place where we try to keep it nice and clean. We got a comment the other day from someone who didn't even know Skylar. The person went to that memorial site, and was scared at first but they got out of the car and felt Skylar, they felt at ease and calm. That made me cry."

Together, Dave and Mary work to make sure the little area stays cared for.

A lot has been said about how trauma and tragedy can tear relationships apart. Increased stress, prolonged court proceedings, financial strain, grief, and depression can all have detrimental impact on a family unit or in a marriage, but it can also be what pulls people together in a time of crisis.

"I read on the internet that 91 percent of families that this thing happens to ends up in divorce. Now that's a high, high number, and for me and Mary to go against the odds," Dave said, "I think that it just shows that we truly love one another, or we couldn't have done this."

Suffering a tragedy can open one's eyes to things that others might not see; one becomes more sensitive in certain areas. In Dave and Mary's case, they became concerned with missing and abducted children cases. Mary shared with me that in the early days of Skylar's disappearance, she learned about all of the stories that were not getting the same media attention that her daughter was receiving.

"You feel guilty because her case is getting so much attention and you read in the newspaper that another little girl was missing in West Virginia, at the same time this was going on with Skylar, like two counties away, maybe a hundred and fifty miles away from us, and no one even knew about it."

Mary would ask people, "'You know this girl? Have you heard anything about the other missing case?'" But no one knew who she was talking about.

"It totally blows my mind that Skylar's was so high profile. I've asked several people along the way, 'Why is this one so big? How did this happen?' And the only response I can get from anybody, and that's from everybody I've asked, was that she was so pretty. She was so beautiful and when people looked at her, they just fell in love with her—it's those beautiful eyes. And that's really sad for the other person out there and the same things happening that they get no attention at all."

In fact, that growing concern for others would be the impetus behind Dave going before West Virginia's legislators and successfully pushing for "Skylar's Law," which expands the Amber Alert legislation by mandating local law enforcement contact state police at the start of any missing-child or child-abduction investigation.

And while most people were focusing on drones, Ebola, the Sony hacks, or whatever else was in the news on a particular day, Dave told me Mary had gone from being concerned about other missing children to making it her mission to post missing-person cases around the area on the internet. "Mary posts girls and boys that are missing. We do pay a lot more attention to that now."

As far as healing is concerned, Mary said, "The media haven't really been bothering us lately, which to me is a godsend, but the pain is still there, it's like it was yesterday. It'll be a while. Truthfully, I don't think it ever will go away. How could it?"

They both continue to work while managing their grief.

"We're just basically working every day and just doing our own little life stuff," Dave said.

Skylar's parents plan to speak more at high schools and especially middle schools. They want kids to learn what happened to Skylar "so we can stop it from ever happening to anybody else again."

In fact, on the day before our conversation, Dave and Mary went to talk to students at a local high school about what happened to their family.

"It was the first time we've done that; we talked to the kids about knowing who your friends are, and about trust," he said.

"And about drugs and stuff like that. I tell you what, it was the best two hours of my life so far. Those kids sat there, and listened. One of them cried with us."

Feeling like a kindred spirit, I told them I'm sometimes exhausted after speaking—that my heart just can't take anymore hurt, because there's so much darkness in the world. It becomes a big part of me; sometimes I wish I could go back to being a little naïve about what the world is like.

Mary said, "Yes, sometimes we just need to be over it. I'm tired . . . we need to be done with it. But then you get that phone call from someone needing help and you think, it can't be over, you can't say no. You just can't do it."

SCARLETT LEWIS

Mother of six-year-old
Newtown tragedy victim
Jesse Lewis

December 14, 2012

Top: Jesse at the beach, September 2011. *Bottom:* Scarlett and Jesse, June 2011, at Scarlett's mother's house in Maine.

M ore than anything else, Scarlett Lewis loved being a mom to her two boys, Jesse, six, and his big brother JT, then twelve.

"A day in our life was getting up early and getting the boys ready for school. That year, JT was getting on the bus at 6:30 in the morning."

Once JT was off to school, Scarlett would feed the chickens, horses, and dogs at the farm they lived on near Newtown, Connecticut.

"Then, I would have an hour with Jesse before I dropped him off to school. He usually slept in bed with me every night. My dad says I shouldn't tell people that, but I am so grateful for that time that we had."

Since losing Jesse, who was one of twenty first-graders and six educators killed in the Sandy Hook Elementary School massacre on December 14, 2012, Scarlett has been very open with the public about the details of her loss. Vivacious, with long blonde hair and an artist's spirit, forty-six-year-old Scarlett found that no detail was too small to share, like how she used to wake Jesse up every morning with a kiss or a song, and then the two of them would "twestle."

"That's tickling and wrestling put together, a word that Jesse made up." At night she read the boys books, like World War II story *Unbroken* and *Tuesdays with Morrie*, about a journalist and his dying mentor. Weekends were just for fun: "In the morning, I would literally Google 'fun stuff to do in Connecticut' and then we were up and out, early."

They'd do a month's worth of activities in one day, hitting a museum, the beach, going to see beagle puppies and then home for a movie and dinner of hot dogs and macaroni and cheese.

Come Monday, the week would start all over again.

On December 13, the last day she'd ever see Jesse alive, Scarlett bundled him up before sending him off with his father, Neil Heslin, who was taking him to school. Jesse had also planned to spend the night with his dad, though he would see his mother at school the next afternoon to make gingerbread. When Scarlett turned to give her son a kiss, she noticed Jesse had written her a message with his finger on the frosted passenger-side of her car window: "I love you."

Scarlett thought the gesture was so sweet, and so Jesse; she ran in the house to get her camera to take a photograph.

It would be the last photograph of him.

On the morning of December 14, Jesse headed to Sandy Hook Elementary with his father. They stopped by the Misty Vale Deli for Jesse's favorite breakfast: a sausage, egg, and cheese sandwich and a cup of hot chocolate. Before parting ways with his father, Jesse hugged and patted him. "It'll be alright, Dad," Jesse said, for no apparent reason. It was 8:50 a.m.

At about that same time, Scarlett was settling in at her job at a software communication firm, where she was the CEO's executive assistant. An hour later, she received a text from a friend, 'You hear about a shooting at a school in Newtown?'

Minutes later, every telephone and electronic gadget was ringing or buzzing around her. By the time Scarlett drove to the school, it was total chaos. Media trucks and emergency rescue vehicles were everywhere, clogging the street. She got out of the car, intending to run toward the school, but was directed by police to the town firehouse, just a mile away from the school.

Nervous and confused, Scarlett waded through hundreds of parents either uniting with their children or calling out their missing child's name. She scanned the crowd for Jesse and his classmates. When someone said several children, including Jesse, might have escaped to a little yellow house about one hundred yards from school, she rushed to check, but the owner said the children had been taken to the nearby daycare. *Thank God*, she thought. But her hopes were dashed once she found out Jesse wasn't among them. She returned to the firehouse, where the mood was becoming more intense by the moment.

"All of us, including my mom, Bob—my stepfather—and my brothers and their wives, were at the firehouse. I remember thinking, *We need peace.* All the parents were upset; there were some yelling and screaming. Nobody was giving us any answers. It was just 'If your kid is missing, write their name down on a list.' Hours and hours went by. I didn't want to be in that room; to me, it was just chaos there. I wanted to create a space of peace for my family. We went outside; we were sitting in the parking lot behind the firehouse. Every time I tried to move away, police officers would say, 'You're in line of sight of the media, you need to get back, more towards the back of the building.' And we did. We didn't want to be in the line of sight of the media."

Hours after the shooting, there was still a lot of misinformation being relayed to the public. Some of the facts were very wrong, since documented by dozens of news reports, a book on the Newtown killings, and several journalistic investigations into the errors, as well as a close look at old social media accounts. The most egregious error hit the airwaves at 2:11 p.m., when major news outlets reported twenty-four-year-old Ryan Lanza (the real shooter's older brother) was allegedly the person responsible for the massacre.

About ten minutes later, several other outlets, going on a tip from a law-enforcement source, followed suit; soon CNN, BuzzFeed, Gawker, Huffington Post, and others were reporting Ryan was the suspect.

As this was being widely reported, Ryan Lanza, an accountant, was watching the drama from a television in the Ernst & Young office in Times Square, where he worked. When he saw himself identified as the shooter on CNN, he left the office in a rush before taking a bus to his apartment building in Hoboken, New Jersey, all the while pleading his case on Facebook: "It wasn't me. I was at work. It wasn't me." And then, "Fuck you, CNN. It's not me."

After getting death threats, he told everyone on Facebook to "Shut the Fuck up." In the midst of all the confusion, another real-time horror was happening to Ryan. His father Peter later told the *New Yorker* that he too saw the news reports that Ryan had committed the killings, but he said he knew better, and immediately assumed it was his younger son, Adam. Peter called Ryan, who reportedly wrote in a text to a friend, "It's my brother. I think my mother is dead. Oh my God!"

By the time Ryan got to his apartment in Hoboken at around 3 p.m., police had roped off the area and were waiting for him; he raised his hands and said, "You're looking for me, but I didn't do it."

He was handcuffed, detained and brought to the Hoboken Police department, where nearly twenty reporters awaited.

At 3:09 p.m., news reports were saying Ryan's mother was dead. At 3:22 p.m., reports claimed "the shooter's brother" was found dead in his Hoboken apartment. Ryan's Facebook profile photo was now all over the internet. By 3:51 p.m., additional erroneous reports ricocheted from the reporters' notebooks to the public: there were two shooters, Ryan's girlfriend's body had been discovered in his Hoboken apartment, Ryan had come to Sandy Hook Elementary to kill his mother, who was a teacher there.

By this point, anybody watching television or scrolling the internet or social media had learned that children had been killed, but, Scarlett said, the parents of the twenty missing first-graders still weren't told until after 4 p.m. At the firehouse, the families were hearing a few rumors, but mostly they were holding onto hope, waiting for officials, who had to keep them in the dark until they were able to verify the victims.

"This will show you what chaos there was," Scarlett said. "There were first responders, there were army men, FBI—all of these people are all over the place. And then this guy, this unmarked guy, comes over kneeling in front of me and says,

'They're over there saying your kid is dead,' and walks away. And then the police come over and ask me, 'What did that guy just say to you?' I said, 'He just told me that Jesse is dead.' They said, 'He's not supposed to say that to you.' They then went and apprehended him and cuffed him." The man, Scarlett would later learn, was some kind of trauma expert, who made a living traveling from one tragedy to the next.

Eventually, it would be a doctor who knelt down beside her and gave her the news officially: *Your son is dead.*

Scarlett couldn't move, not a finger, until she heard her older son JT start to cry. She then grabbed him and wouldn't let him go.

By 5:45 p.m., CNN and the Associated Press were reporting several significant mistakes had been made in earlier reporting: The AP said a law enforcement source had accidentally transposed the names of the brothers, naming Ryan as the shooter. Nancy Lanza, Ryan's mother, wasn't a teacher at Sandy Hook Elementary School, but she *was* dead. It was Ryan's younger brother, Adam, who allegedly shot her and then killed the children and educators at the school before killing himself.

Sometime before 9:30 that Friday morning, December 14, twenty-year-old Adam left his mother's 3,100-square-foot colonial home, where he had just fatally shot her in her sleep. He then drove to Sandy Hook Elementary, which he attended as a child. Pointing his rifle at the entrance window, he shattered the glass with bullets and then walked through the large hole. The entire tragedy, from the moment the glass shattered until Adam turned the gun on himself, took less than five minutes.

In the immediate aftermath, the rush for the media to be first created another victim in a tragedy that already had far too many. Though the reporting errors were publicly clarified, damage had already been done. As one media outlet said, "For a few brief hours, social media users brought the digital equivalent of pitchfork and torches" to bear on an innocent young man.

As evening settled, more information was coming out about what happened inside Sandy Hook Elementary. Despite all the pain Scarlett was feeling, she wasn't surprised when an investigator later told her of Jesse's heroics. By the time Adam Lanza entered Jesse's first-grade classroom, he had already opened fire, killing the principal, the school psychologist, several teachers, and many young children. The first person he shot in Jesse's class was Victoria Soto, Jesse's favorite teacher. Jesse yelled for the students to "Run now!" while Adam reloaded his gun. Four boys did just that, running right past the shooter to safety. Jesse was doomed; the gunman shot several of his classmates and the young hero in the forehead.

That evening, the media camped out in front of Scarlett's farmhouse, but she and her surviving son, JT, were across town at her mother's home.

"That's why I can say they were not intrusive. The other families have horror stories of reporters hiding in the woods and things like that. I didn't have that because they didn't know where I was.

"But my friends did say there was one incident. There were lots of people at my home trying to coordinate help for all the animals at the farm. During that time, someone had knocked on my door and a woman came in, holding a plant and said, 'I am one of Scarlett's dear friends from high school and I just wanted to know where and when the funeral is?' And of course the funeral is private and we were trying to keep it that way because we didn't want that information to go public. My friends said, 'Sure, absolutely,' and gave her the information for the funeral. She left, and they looked at the card she handed them. It was someone from one of the major networks. My friend called me in horror. 'We were tricked. You're going to kill us.' I said, 'Oh my gosh, don't worry; that could have happened to me. How could you possibly know?'"

Emotionally and physically exhausted, Scarlett wanted nothing but rest. "My stepfather gave me a sleeping pill. I knew I needed to sleep. JT was crying; we went up to bed and we talked for a little bit and then we fell asleep together."

Still in shock as the effects of the sleeping pill wore off the next morning, Scarlett fixed a cup of tea and checked her mobile phone.

"Jesse's father had sent me a text: 'Jesse is being eulogized on the cover of the *New York Post*.' I remember thinking, *What? Why? That's odd. I don't understand. Why would they—*" Then she realized the nightmare was real.

"I'll never forget this. The cover of the *New York Post*, I counted twenty-six people, twenty children. I saw Jesse's face and fell to the ground and I started bawling. I could not believe the magnitude of the tragedy. I knew that Jesse was a part of it, but I couldn't believe that there were so many others. I had no idea. I remember thinking, *I'm not ... I can't ... I know my limits of what I can handle and what I can't and I can't go online and look things up. I can't do it.*"

I can't help but try and understand what it was like for this small, close-knit town, now exposed on a very large screen. Grieving in private wasn't an option since, by the end of the day, nearly two hundred reporters and photographers from around the world would end up in Newtown, capturing its residents' most vulnerable moments: scared children running out of the school in the conga-style line students had learned during safety drills weeks earlier; a father running aimlessly to find answers; a sister breaking down as she finds out her sibling is dead; burly emergency workers crumbling to the ground after seeing the carnage inside the school.

Shortly after the shootings, about the same time the twenty-six families were beginning to plan funerals, local politicians implored reporters to leave town. Even the staff of the local daily newspaper, the *Newtown Bee*, literally begged fellow journalists in a Facebook post and tweets to "STAY AWAY FROM THE VICTIMS," saying that it was time to go.

But the public's desire for more stories out of Newtown proved too great for reporters to stay away. Reporters also descended on Stamford, Connecticut, where Peter Lanza, the shooter's father, lived and on Nancy Lanza's hometown in New Hampshire.

No one denies the media can sometimes cause additional pain for the surviving families, but Scarlett decided early on that rather than dodge media questions, she would talk publicly in order to keep Jesse's memory alive. She told reporters over and over about her son's heroics, and about her own grieving process.

She believes the media played an important role in the healing process. She told me the stories the reporters wrote and aired helped inspire compassion from across the world. People wanted to hear how Newtown was coping, and the best way to do that, according to Scarlett, was through the media. Her relationship with the press was the opposite of my own, so I was especially interested in how it began, there in the midst of her grief.

The day after the tragedy, the reporters discovered Scarlett was hiding out at her mother's house.

"I'm not sure how they found my mother's number, but it took them two days, and they were calling for interviews. Within the first couple of weeks it was Oprah and Anderson Cooper. I didn't talk to them."

I wanted to know more: When did she decide to talk? Did Scarlett's family make the decision on who should be the family spokesperson or did somebody choose her? Did anyone from law enforcement reach out to say, 'This is going to happen to you; let us help you'?

"Nothing like that," she said, before explaining to me how she started talking to the media in the midst of her grief:

"I remember Trent, my brother, coming up and saying, 'It's *People* magazine.' Trent said his friend Max had a cousin at *People* magazine who wants to talk to me.' And I would look at him and go, 'NO! NO! I don't want to talk to anybody.'"

She said it was the third time that her brother came to her with the phone that she finally listened. "Trent had the phone, and said 'They want to talk to you, and the reporter promises she is going to be respectful.'"

Scarlett recalls her brother saying, "'And I'm just going say this, if you don't talk to *People* magazine, I think they are going to talk to someone else.' I remember just going, 'Give me the phone.'"

She walked up to her mother's room and took a deep breath: "I said, 'Hi, how are you? Let's talk.' It was coming from me and not someone else. That's why I started to talk to the media."

During those early days, Scarlett had no idea the world was following the tragedy so closely, until President Obama came to Newtown High School on December 17 to address the nation and meet the families.

"Then I knew it was a very public thing. I had no expectations about the president's meeting. I said, 'I want you to know that Jesse acted very bravely during his last few minutes and he was instrumental in saving the lives of his classmates.' He said, 'May I see that?'"—referring to the picture of Jesse on Scarlett's cell phone. Obama took the phone and closely looked at Jesse's photograph.

"He said, 'I can tell by looking at your son's face that you weren't surprised at his brave actions.' I said, 'You're right. I wasn't surprised.' I really didn't hear his speech. I was crying the whole time, with my head on JT's shoulder."

Healing was an ongoing process to Scarlett, which has included therapy with a counselor, as well as alternative therapies like tapping, a combination of ancient acupressure and psychology, and Reiki, a Japanese technique for stress reduction. She also held onto her Christian faith, and spent precious time with the other grieving parents. Her journey even led her to meeting the Dalai Lama.

But she said messages she believed were left by Jesse are what really helped her get by. Sometimes the signs were as simple as a flickering light, and other times they were more divine. During a trip to Florida, Scarlett and JT were driving along an unfamiliar road to the hotel when they looked up. A small engine plane had written a message in the sky. "Jesse and Jesus together forever." It was especially amazing, said Scarlett, since no one knew where they were and she had just expressed to her son that "Jesse is with Jesus."

But it was one particular sign that changed everything for Scarlett. "There was this message on my kitchen chalkboard."

Shortly before Jesse's death, he had scribbled three words on a chalkboard: *nurturing, healing, love.*

"I knew instantly when I saw it that this was my life purpose, that I had to spread this message, and that those three words—nurturing, healing, love—were powerful enough to heal."

Inspired by Jesse's heartfelt scribblings, she started the Jesse Lewis Choose Love Foundation, which creates compassion- and wisdom-based curriculums for schools. When President Obama met with the families again at Hartford University, she quickly mentioned her new foundation to him. He connected her to his sister, who runs a similar foundation.

"I began to speak publicly because I wanted that message [nurturing, healing, love] to get out there. I was Jesse's mouthpiece. I rallied quickly. The first time I made a public appearance was at the safety commission meeting in Newtown at the Newtown High School."

About eight hundred people showed up. Scarlett was prepared to discuss her new foundation, and how she was on a mission to promote social emotional learning in schools, teaching kids how to effectively deal with their anger so that it doesn't become destructive. But when a number of speakers spent their time reviewing gun clips that could be banned, she almost shied away.

"I remember telling my dad, 'This isn't the forum to be talking about choosing love,' and he said, 'This is exactly the forum to be talking about choosing love.'"

She got a standing ovation, which let her know she was doing the right thing for little Jesse and the other children who died at Newtown.

"I thought, 'This is what we need.' I believe that if our school had a social emotional component to the teaching when Adam went to school there, the tragedy would have never happened."

Six months after the shooting, she wrote an e-book, *Nurturing Healing Love: A Mother's Journey of Hope and Forgiveness.* Scarlett believes she had divine assistance from God and Jesse to help her along the way as she wrote and began her crusade.

Her son JT's suffering was also channeled into something positive. Less than a month after Jesse's death, several young Rwandan genocide survivors reached out to JT through Skype.

"At this point, we were completely alone in the house; JT hadn't gone to school and I hadn't gone back to work yet. We were suffering and not moving forward and these beautiful, young Rwandan kids gave us strength. They basically said we suffered and we want you to hear our story so that you know that you will be okay and that you will feel joy again."

Inspired by their stories, JT started his own organization called Newtown Helps Rwanda. He threw himself into fundraising for the Rwandan survivors, and raised money for one of them to attend college.

Having been exposed to so many high-profile stories and families over the years, I have always been encouraged when the media choses to "lay a little lower" when children victims are involved versus when someone is of age, though I always find myself wondering why *only* for child victims. Shouldn't we extend as much restraint and sensitivity as we can to *every* victim?

Although the media exercised tact and compassion in Newtown, still I wondered: Did Scarlett feel the message she wanted to share about Jesse was always delivered the way she envisioned? Did the media handle her respectfully or did they tweak and tailor her message to fit their needs?

She began to tell me about how the first television story about her fundraiser came about:

"I remember I was home with one of my board of directors. There was a guy outside my house that I've never seen before. I said, 'Excuse me?' He said, 'This is all I want to say to you, I know that you have a mission.' He said, 'I know that you probably have a negative idea about the media, but I want to help you with your mission. If you wanted to announce the foundation you created and Jesse's message, or anything that you want to say, I will offer my services and my station.'"

Scarlett looked at the journalist, who was from NBC, in the eye, and decided he was trustworthy. "I said, 'You know what, come in. I think, maybe, I am ready to announce it.'" He came in, but my board of director was very savvy and railed him out and said, 'Get the heck out of here! How dare you come into this house?!'"

Despite the concern expressed by her colleague, the next day she called the reporter back to her home. He promptly returned with a cameraman. Not only did he air a story about the foundation, but when Scarlett needed him to raise money for a family who lost two children when a drunk driver crashed into the car, the reporter produced a three-part series.

But were there journalists, I wondered, who promised to help, but did not come through after they had gotten their story?

"My experience with the media, aside from that one incident, has been very positive," she said. "If they are attending a function that I'm attending, and they've heard me speak, they'll say, 'We want to help you get your message across.' They have never twisted my words and when I tell them I won't comment on something, they always respect my wishes. I've never been unhappy with an article."

She told me she learned to answer questions not unlike a politician. "You answer how you want to answer. I knew they weren't going to correct me live in front of their viewers because that would make them look like assholes."

Scarlett learned a very important lesson about interviews, and fairly quickly: don't let the media push you into saying something you'll later regret. Scarlett's choice to be extremely open to the media in telling her story also gave reporters no reason to dig around or conjure up stories.

But not everyone in Newtown felt the same way about letting the outside world in. As the one-year mark of the Sandy Hook tragedy approached in 2013, the town was not interested in the media invading Newtown yet again.

In fact, Patricia Llodra, the town's first selectman (equivalent to a mayor), told the press there would be no memorial services and urged the media to stay away. She asked churches, institutions, and businesses not to let television outlets park their vans in their parking lots. Police kept an eye out for television trucks parked on smaller roads. Those who dared defy Llodra's request had to tread very lightly.

Many journalists from large organizations promised they would not come to Newtown and instead covered the tragedy from a distance, so they had to work a little harder to find appropriate stories. Without a memorial service, print and television reporters couldn't rely on the standard photographs of flickering candlelight casting a glow on tearful faces.

The parents of the children who survived the shooting worried the media would just cause more anxiety for their families, and were quoted in newspapers as saying that, while the journalists they'd encountered in Newtown had been very respectful, the families still deserved privacy.

Scarlett disagreed with the town officials' decision to have no part of the media.

"I was in the minority, but I felt like the media should have been invited. In my mind the media wanted to come because the world was mourning with us and wanted to know how we were doing. This was a way for the world to find out."

Since they were not officially invited to Newtown, many of the news outlets called Scarlett to see if she had something to say on her own.

"I said, 'Absolutely, I do. Come to my house.' They were like, 'Okay, well, we're not allowed in town.'" I said, 'I'm inviting you to my private property.'"

Her house was full of activity; there was a live broadcast and every day three different networks from different countries would file in and file out.

Scarlett said reporters were kind and respectful, and wanted to know how she was doing. They'd say, "'So sorry for your loss.' And, 'Our viewers want to know how you got through this year.' I knew the people watching wanted to honor our loss by being a part of it, and I was wanting that too."

COLLENE CAMPBELL

Sister of murdered NASCAR
driver Mickey Thompson

March 16, 1988

Top left: One of the last photos of Trudy and Mickey, with their dog Punkie. Collene took this picture, just feet away from where the couple would be killed months later. *Top right:* Collene, Gary, and their cockatoo, Babe, on Collene and Gary's sixtieth wedding anniversary. Babe was an earlier gift from the entire family, given to celebrate the couple's thirty years of marriage. *Bottom:* One of the last Campbell family photos taken with Scott before he died. From left to right: Shelly, Gary, Collene, and Scott.

I t was a long, beautiful drive to meet Collene Campbell, sister to NASCAR legend and promoter Mickey Thompson. Her home, completely secluded, sits inside a stunning, gated community, with tall billowing trees surrounding it like a blanket, a scene out of a storybook. I drove slowly up the long winding road, to the dead-end street, to find her standing there, waving me in.

"Collene, this place is phenomenal; I am in awe," I blurted out before even putting my car in park.

Collene smiled brightly at me. "Well, with all the death threats I get, this is where I feel the safest."

Collene was taught at a very young age how to protect herself. Some of her fondest childhood memories are from the shooting range with her father, the former chief of detectives for the Alhambra Police Department in Southern California, who'd take her with him for target practice. Dressed in the cutest little fluffy dress, her hair all done up in curls, she'd stand alongside him, ready to take aim.

Laughing to herself, Collene, now in her eighties, told me her father, who was also captain of the police pistol team, just loved to brag that she was better than some of the officers.

"He'd get the biggest kick out of it," she boasted.

She and her older brother Mickey were three and a half years apart, but inseparable.

"He was my best friend." Collene was with him when their parents drove to the Bonneville Salt Flats in Utah for the first time, where years later Mickey would shatter race-car records. Back then, the determined little seven-year old declared to his family that he was going to break the world record and become the "fastest person in the world."

"He wanted to bring the trophy home," Collene recalls. And when he did in 1960, achieving international fame and breaking a world record after driving his Challenger 1 to a top speed of 406.60 mph, Collene was right there to celebrate with him.

The same steely determination that big brother Mickey had used to build the world's fastest car from four used Pontiac engines, Collene had in bucketloads. But for much of her life, her resolve was focused on a different objective: hunting down the cold-blooded killers who destroyed her family, robbing her of her son, Scotty, and less than five years later, her brother, Mickey.

It would take Collene months to connect the dots from the last known whereabouts of her son Scotty to his vicious killers. It would take nearly nineteen years, and everything she learned during her son's case, to send the man who ordered a hit on her famous brother and his wife, Trudy, to prison for life.

She stared at me, pensive. "Gary and I have been married for sixty-three years, but more than half of our married life we've been going through all of this murder stuff."

Gary and Collene were childhood sweethearts. "Did you know we met in second grade? Later, I worked with my brother, doing his public relations, and Gary was in publishing."

The life they created for themselves felt perfect. "It was heaven," she continued. "And we have a wonderful daughter, Shelley, and we had a wonderful son, Scotty. He was an electronics genius, he built stuff to help Mickey in his car."

As Collene talked about Scotty, it was like she was describing my brother, Ron: handsome, gregarious, energetic smile; both struggling to find their way, dabbling in a lot of different things, waiting for something to click.

On April 17, 1982, Scotty, who was twenty-nine years old at the time, vanished. "Eleven months it took us to find out what happened to him," Collene said. She inhaled deeply before continuing on.

"The man who murdered my son, Larry Cowell, came from a very good family; they were actually friends of ours. He was in trouble quite a bit . . . I felt very bad for the parents because they kept trying to make excuses for him. The day that Scotty was going to see him, I said, 'Where are you going, honey?' He said, 'Mom, I'm going to go see Larry.' I said, 'Scotty, he's in all kinds of trouble, why would you do that?' I never saw him again."

That day, the unsuspecting Scotty boarded a private jet rented by Cowell, who also served as pilot. Donald DiMascio, the man Cowell hired to kill Scotty, was hiding behind Scotty's seat; just after takeoff, he appeared. Recordings from the flight revealed Cowell and DiMascio laughing about how they bloodied him up so the sharks could eat him, before they strangled him, broke his neck, and threw him out of the plane, nearly 2,000 feet above the Pacific Ocean. News reports claimed the elaborate plot to kill Scotty was revenge for a previous drug deal gone bad.

Describing the three murder trials she endured to get justice for her son, Collene said, "It was seven years, nine months, and nine days; the longest funeral you have ever been to."

There were no news reports surrounding Scotty's disappearance, his death, or murder trials, not unlike thousands of other victims who go missing or are murdered; not every family's story gets told.

But that privacy would change for this family less than five years after Scotty's disappearance, when right in the middle of the retrial for one of Scotty's killers, Collene and Gary would be confronted with another murder mystery, one that would take nearly two decades to solve.

On March 16, 1988, Collene thought her biggest concern was her daughter Shelley, who was struggling to get through a very dangerous pregnancy. Mickey and Trudy were going to the hospital to see their niece.

"They were going to stop by their office first, and they were taking Shelley her favorite breakfast, so they were up very early that morning. I will never forget it because Mickey called me every morning at 6 a.m; we were so close, but that morning I hadn't heard from him yet."

At 6:05 a.m., Mickey and Trudy were on their way to the office at their stadium-racing business when two hooded men on ten-speed bicycles met them at the driveway.

"It was a mean kill. You knew it was revenge. They didn't steal anything. Trudy tried to run," Collene said. "There was a witness, a little young girl, who saw them bring Trudy over to where Mickey was. He had already been shot in the arm at this point, and he was heard yelling, 'Don't shoot my wife!' Still, they brought her over to Mickey and put the bullet in her head. They brought her close so Mickey could see; Mickey was still yelling, 'Don't hurt my wife!'" Two different neighbors heard him screaming. "He had five bullets in him when he died. And the two killers rode off on their bicycles, and we never found them."

As Collene took me through those final moments of her big brother's life, detailing how he pleaded with their killers not to kill Trudy, "his baby," I got chills.

The horrific images I've seen in photographs of the couple's lifeless bodies lying on the driveway tugged at my mind. But what Collene said next snapped me back to her story.

"Our daughter Shelly, who was waiting for them at the hospital, was watching *Good Morning America*, when suddenly pictures of Trudy and Mickey in the driveway, dead, appeared on the screen. And she calls me on the phone and she says, 'Please tell me this is not true.' And I didn't know what to say, she's just trying to save her baby and she sees it on television, on *Good Morning America!*"

By this point, Collene had already learned that something horrible had happened. "I received a call from Mickey's neighbor and he said something's happened at their house. I immediately called the sheriff's department and I said, 'This is Collene

Thompson Campbell, Mickey Thompson's sister.' And he says, 'Just a moment, please.' He put me on hold and came back and that was it. Gary was still lying in bed and I went over to him and said, 'Another horrible pain, Mickey and Trudy have been killed.' And I never will forget it. 'We've got to go over there.'"

Collene began to tremble, though she wanted to finish the story. Despite how often a survivor tells their story, it can still feel like the first time, every time.

The murders made news all over the world:

"Racer-Promoter Mickey Thompson and Wife Slain Outside Their Home," and "Racing King's Death Unsolved: Stack of Clues Leads Nowhere in the Mickey Thompson Slayings."

Some very disturbing rumors from well-meaning citizens followed. Could Thompson's fame have made him a target of a jealous competitor or angry fan? Was he the victim of drug dealers wanting to deliver a "don't mess with us" message?

"Absolutely not," Collene said. Police agreed, quickly ruling out drugs, robbery, or extramarital affair. They knew only one thing for sure: it was an assassination.

Three days before the murders, Mickey told Collene something she'd never forget.

"He said, 'Sis, I am really concerned.' Mickey had never said he was concerned about anything; he's a guy that gets in a car and goes four hundred miles an hour. He's not concerned. I said, 'What's the matter, Mick?' He said, 'I am really concerned about Goodwin hurting my baby.' I said, 'There's no way, Mick.' He says, 'Collene, I'm telling you, this guy is capable of it and I feel it in my bones.' Three days later he's dead, so I knew exactly who did it."

Michael Goodwin, a rival promoter, was a onetime business partner of Mickey back in the 1980s. Together they promoted stadium motocross events, but their relationship turned sour over a bitter financial dispute, which landed them in court.

Shortly after the California Supreme Court affirmed a $531,000 court judgment in Mickey's favor, Goodwin filed bankruptcy. And roughly one year later, Mickey and Trudy were dead.

Over the years, stories of Mickey's unsolved murder, and Collene's fight for justice, would be featured on shows like *Unsolved Mysteries, Murder by the Book, 48 Hours,* and *America's Most Wanted.* The *CSI* fourth-season episode "Early Rollout" was even based on his murder case.

"I never sought any of it out. They called me and I said as long as we can stick to the facts it's okay," Collene told me.

Most of us thrust into the spotlight are like deer caught in headlights, but Collene knew how to handle the media and make her dealings with them work to her advantage.

"I had more experience with it, because I had handled all of Mickey's publicity in racing for years. I had handled the media and the photographers and in a positive way. Since I had been involved in the racing world, that may have helped some."

Calculating that it was easier to make change from within, Collene became San Juan Capistrano's first female mayor in 1992 after serving on the city council for seven years; she was elected as mayor again in 2000. Collene says her biggest accomplishment during her tenure was seeing crime drop 74 percent.

But it was the organization she and her husband Gary began at the gravesite of her brother that would be her legacy: MOVE (Memory of Victims Everywhere), a foundation that works to change laws to benefit crime victims. Her efforts would help put in place two important pieces of reform: In June 1990, California voters passed the Crime Victims Justice Reform Act, which included expanding the definition of first-degree murder and allowing hearsay evidence from victims during pre-trial hearings. And on October 30, 2004, President George W. Bush signed into federal law the Scott Campbell [et al] Crime Victims Rights Act, which guarantees crime victims the right to be present at and notified of all proceedings, the right to restitution, the right to a speedy trial, the right to safety, and, most important, the right to be heard.

Yet while she fought to secure rights for victims across the country, her personal quest for justice never wavered. Mickey and Trudy remained her motivation to stay focused and determined.

Collene is featured prominently throughout a *48 Hours* special on Mickey and Trudy's unsolved deaths that aired in 2002. Standing at five-foot-two, neatly dressed like a politician, with her blondish brown hair perfectly coifed, her gentle smile identical to Mickey's, and her eyes unrelenting, she was a cross between Queen Elizabeth and Annie Oakley.

"Is Michael Goodwin guilty? You're darn right Michael Goodwin is guilty," she says. Later, looking steadily into the camera, her eyes slightly squinting, she says, "If he killed my brother, then I want him brought to justice. And," she promises, "I'll do everything in my power to make that happen."

An LA county sheriff who worked with Collene on her son's murder case tells *48 Hours*, "Yes sir, she's a hell of a detective."

Another officer, this time Sheriff's Detective Mark Lillienfeld, who worked closely with Gary and Collene on Mickey's case, describes her as "a grieving, pissed off elderly woman who lost a brother and sister-in-law that she loved dearly. She was someone with fire in her belly."

But it isn't just police officers giving Collene their praise in the *48 Hours* segment; so did members of the media. A CBS producer calls her "a force of nature . . . instrumental in keeping attention focused on the unsolved murder of her brother and sister-in-law."

Using a NASCAR metaphor, savvy Collene tells a *48 Hours'* reporter, "It's been an endurance race that Gary and I, and my family, are sticking to, racing it out, doing the best we can to bring justice to our family."

While many survivors often try to keep from crying in front of the camera, fearing they might look weak or that the reporter was trying to take advantage of them, Collene was just herself, often caught tearing up. And yet, she was always described as being tough as nails.

"If you lock horns with Collene, you will not win," a detective tells the correspondent on the *48 Hours* segment.

Her voice cracks only once during the interview, when the reporter asks her to describe her son. She looks stunned for a moment, and then weary, and sighs before smiling. "Twenty years and I still can't talk about it."

The cameras follow Collene and Gary into a sprawling garden as they prune larges roses and place them in a basket. "This one is definitely for Mickey and Trudy," she says, handing the rose to her husband. The scene cuts to the couple walking through a cemetery, where Collene softly cries, while wrapped in her husband's embrace.

Anyone thinking Collene would be too mentally exhausted to keep fighting, day after day for nearly fifteen years straight, would have sorely underestimated her, especially once Mickey and Collene's ailing mother, Geneva, asked her daughter to make her a promise.

"Kim, see this little thing I have around my neck?" Collene asked, holding the necklace toward me. "My mom hit ninety-six years old and that was several years after Mick and Trudy were killed. Police still hadn't made the arrest yet, and she was dying. She said to me, 'I want you to take my necklace off and I want you to wear it until they get the person that killed your brother and my son. Please don't take it off.' I said, 'I can't take that necklace, Daddy gave it to you.' She said, 'I want you to take it off and put it on.' So I did, and then it didn't come off until they got him. And now, I wear it all the time."

I understood completely; I made a similar promise in my brother's memory: that I would never stop until justice was served for his murder.

Collene curses worse than a sailor and packs heat, but her tenderness is never out of arms' reach. And if she happens to cry, instead of looking weak, Collene still somehow appears composed—a person who's had to endure too much, and for too long. Maybe that's why people like her so much. Maybe that's why I admire her.

Truthfully, I think Collene was too preoccupied with the task at hand, keeping her brother's case alive, to care how she was being perceived by the media. I really couldn't get a straight answer about her feelings toward those reporters who covered her case.

"Can you remember a time when a reporter . . ." "Did the media ever . . ." Shaking her head no each time before I even finished my sentence, she said she didn't watch the news, doesn't surf the internet, and is not active on social media. It was never about her, or being on TV, or being in the limelight; it was and is always about her son, her brother, her mission to seek justice.

Despite her apparent lack of concern with the coverage, Collene worked the media with grace and ease. Investigative reporters at some of the largest newspapers, magazines, and television crime shows like *Hard Copy* and *America's Most Wanted* marveled at her skill.

Journalists also were impressed at how well she worked alongside law enforcement, providing names and leads to police officers, without interfering with the case. "Somebody should pin a detective's badge on Collene Thompson Campbell," the *LA Times* wrote in 2010.

"Overall, I think the media has been very good to us and reported things truthfully," Collene told me. But she said there were times when journalists would report untrue things, just because someone said it.

"Especially because Goodwin had direct access to them once he was behind bars. For example, the *Orange County Register* accepted collect calls from him from prison and ran what he said, which was untrue. It put us in a bad light; that was painful. And when I called and raised hell, they said, 'People like to read this.'

California allows criminals to call the newspapers and have access to the internet. They give the media bad stories about victims that hurt victims. But in general, I think that we've had pretty good luck with the media."

Collene wasn't "some housewife" who demanded reporters to write a story about her case, one television reporter would say.

Instead, Collene was known to simply say, "I don't know if you will be interested in this but . . ." In fact, she knew exactly what journalists were interested in, and knew the stories they published would keep her brother's case on everyone's mind; she was especially focused on catching the attention of someone out in the public who might have information to share.

All of her hard work and relationship-building with the media would eventually pay off.

Thirteen years after the killings, the show *America's Most Wanted* broadcasted on Mickey and Trudy's murders triggered the memories of two of Mickey's neighbors, Ron Stevens and his wife, Toni. At the time the crime was committed, the couple told police that several days before the killings, they saw a man sitting in a faded blue station wagon with Arizona tags outside their home. The mystery man, Stevens reported, was looking toward Mickey's home through binoculars.

During the initial investigation, police were so narrowly focused on the two bicycle-riding hit men that they didn't see a link. But more than a decade later, law enforcement finally saw the connection and even brought several photographs to the Stevens' house. The couple identified Goodwin as the man who was sitting in the car. They later picked him out in a police lineup and ultimately he was arrested.

But the media attention and the investigation only fanned the flames between Goodwin and Collene. She continued to try to help her brother's estate collect the long-ago financial judgment of $531,000 that Goodwin was ordered to pay.

She boldly told the *LA Times* that "nothing has changed. The settlement is not going to be handled any differently now than when Mickey and Trudy were alive. I believe we should be paid in full."

She stayed vocal in her belief that Goodwin was guilty of murder, which only provoked Goodwin to threaten her.

In fact, she told me of the countless threats Goodwin made against her, all of which she reported to police. She admits that, at one point, she almost wished he would come for her, just so *she* could end it all herself—a thought I have definitely had as well.

Finally, on January 5, 2007, after nearly nineteen years, a Pasadena jury convicted Michael Goodwin of murdering his former racing-promoter partner and his wife, Trudy. Collene, then seventy-four years old, could begin to breathe a sigh of relief; this cold case was officially closed. Goodwin was sentenced to two consecutive life sentences, without the possibility of parole.

"I wish I could look up and touch Mickey and Trudy and say, 'We won!'" Collene said after the verdict to the gaggle of reporters outside the courtroom, her eyes filled with tears, as she waved a black-and-white checkered racing flag in triumph.

Justice did not come without great sacrifice, an endless supply of perseverance and hope, and an unwavering commitment from Collene and Gary, who spent years before, during, and after the case was resolved as committed victims' advocates, fighting to change laws to protect the rights of families and survivors.

You can see all the hard work the moment you walk into Collene's office, which sits at the end of a long hallway in her home. The space is filled with piles of old newspaper articles, magazines, case files, even a working typewriter.

Pictures adorn the walls, highlighting meetings with President Gerald Ford, President George H.W. Bush, and numerous governors, attorney generals, and senators, alongside awards she has received for years of dedication to the victims' movement.

I stopped to notice two portraits, both painted by Collene: one of Mickey and Trudy, the other of Scotty. They brought tears to my eyes. I could see the time, effort, and love she put into each detail, capturing the essence of her loved ones.

In the background, as we spoke, I could hear the squawking of her beautiful white sulfur-crested triton cockatoo, named Babe, who Collene warned me gets agitated when she does. "She's very protective of me," she said.

Collene and I share a kinship, as the baby sisters who never gave up on trying to protect our brothers' legacies, though we differed in the way we chose to protect ourselves.

As we walked through her house, showcasing all of her accolades as a victim advocate and mayor, Collene—who refers to herself as an old grandma—asked me very casually, "What kind of gun do you have, Kim?"

"Uh, I don't have a weapon. I've shot a gun before, but I don't own one."

She looked at me, exasperated. "What the fuck is wrong with you? A woman in our situation needs protection at all times."

I hadn't really ever felt unsafe in my life, despite the countless death threats I've received over the years. But Collene was more exposed; she was fighting a very public fight against a man she knew was capable of killing.

I asked, has she ever just wanted to walk away from all of this? Though I knew exactly what she would say.

"No, I can't say I have. I have wanted to pound a fist in people's faces but I can't say that I ever wanted to walk away. Every night I pray to God, please help me use my unwanted education to help others in the justice system. I don't feel like I'm making much progress though."

When I asked about the concept of closure, and what she wanted her legacy to be, she validated why I look up to her so much, after all these years.

"I'd love to say that in honor of my murdered family we were able to improve the justice system where other people don't have to hurt quite as deep." But she believes there's much work yet to do. "All of us survivors have gained a set of skills we didn't ask for," Collene said. "We need to use this unwanted education to help others, and improve a broken justice system."

She paused as if shaping what she was about to say.

"Closure is really silly. I'm sure every night when you go to sleep, Kim, you, too, think about this stuff and no matter what you do you can't get it out of your mind," she said. "And I try to think about puppy dogs and kitty cats and all kinds of other things, but when I go to sleep I'm thinking about Mickey and Trudy and Scotty and 'I wish I could have saved them' and I don't think that will ever change."

SCOTT AND KATHLEEN LARIMER

Parents of Aurora theater shooting victim John Larimer

SHIRLEY WYGAL

Mother of Aurora theater shooting victim Rebecca Wingo

July 20, 2012

Top left: John with his siblings, Christmas Eve 2011. From left to right: John, Noel, Anne, Nora, and Beth. *Top right:* John at basic training graduation from Great Lakes Naval Academy, 2011. John was fourth-generation US Navy. *Center:* Kathleen and Scott Larimer, taken the day after John died at Kathleen's grandmother's one-hundredth birthday celebration. "Scott and I had our fake smiles in place."

Left: Rebecca, May 2012. This picture, taken with Shirley's phone, is what Shirley showed reporters to help find her missing daughter hours after the shooting. *Right:* Shirley and Rebecca, Valentine's Day 2012.

It was a Sunday afternoon in 2014, the week after the New England Patriots beat the Seattle Seahawks in Super Bowl XLIX. My father and I are on a conference call, waiting for members of the families impacted by the *Dark Knight Rises* massacre in Aurora, Colorado, on July 20, 2012, which left twelve people dead and scores injured, to join us.

The trial for shooter James Holmes was underway. He'd been charged with twenty-four counts of murder (two counts for every death), 116 counts of attempted murder, possession of explosive devices, and inciting violence. Holmes, who at the time of the killings was a twenty-five-year-old neuroscience student, pled not guilty by reason of insanity. At this stage of the court proceedings, nearly 9,000 prospective jurors were being assembled in Aurora, the largest pool ever to be called in American history.

Since my father and I know a little something about high-profile trials, we were asked by one of the victims' family members to share our experience and our insight as to what these grief-stricken families are likely to endure. They were calling in from all over the country, including Ohio, New York, Illinois, California, and Colorado.

At the start of the call, my father expressed his deepest condolences for the loss of life that everyone had experienced. I echoed his sentiments and thanked them for trusting us in their time of need and suffering.

Then the survivors began to speak. As I listened to the families state their names and claim the memory of their sons, daughters, siblings, and grandchild, my hands started to sweat.

While a conference call may sound cold and informal, in reality it was intimate and emotional. I never expected to feel so connected to a group of strangers in such a quick minute. I could hear their pain, anguish, and struggle. It resonated with me. I remember saying to the group that none of us who've been victimized have ever wanted to be part of this "group," but that I've learned over the years that sometimes there is nothing more comforting than being around people who just get it. Not only did we have a tremendous loss of life in common, but we all had stories that made headlines for weeks and months on end.

I understood how it felt to be thrown into these extreme media environments at the absolute worst time of your life; it's as confusing as it is frightening. No one in their right mind wants to be the center of a tragic news story, but some reporters lose sight of the magnitude of those tragedies and cover them as if they are just another news event.

So it's no surprise the Aurora survivors came with so many concerns and questions: "What kinds of things were you not prepared for?" "What level of involvement did you have with the district attorney's office?" "Did you view the crime scene photos or the autopsy pictures?" "How did you handle yourself with the media?"

There were additional questions that I'm opting not to share, out of respect for the families' privacy; my father and I systematically answered all of them with honesty, compassion, and a lot of tears.

Two of the callers during that ninety-minute conversation were Kathleen and Scott Larimer from Crystal Lake, Illinois, a suburb of Chicago. They are the parents of US Navy Petty Officer Third Class John Larimer, the youngest of five children and one of the twelve people killed in the theater.

Days after the conference call, I talked to them again. Scott, a retired Navy man, had a voice that reminded me of my father's, full of wisdom and heartache. I couldn't help but smile at his affectionate banter with his wife, the loving bond they had with their other children, and the stories they liked to tell about John, who at the time of his death was a cryptologic technician stationed at the US Fleet Cyber Command station at Buckley Air Force Base.

"John's great-grandfather was in the Navy. He was the fifth person in our family to serve in the Navy," Scott said, explaining he had another son in the same service branch.

"He graduated from college while waiting tables at Chili's," John's mother recalled.

"The last time we saw John in the flesh," Scott said, "was the morning of July 2, which is my wife's birthday. Last time we spoke to him was July 16, on my birthday, just a few weeks later."

For a long time after John's death, they kept a voice message from him on the answering machine, but "then we had some kind of mishap and it got erased," Scott said.

"In some ways it's like losing him all over again." Kathleen added.

"As time moved on, I was happy the answering machine had a glitch," Scott went on. "I'm not sure why I would want to keep it."

During our conversation, Scott and Kathleen expressed concerns many times about the upcoming trial and the media coverage that would accompany it. "The area where the cameras are going to be in the courthouse will be restricted, so hopefully the media will follow that," Kathleen said, sighing heavily. "I don't want to worry about the things you worried about, Kim, like checking under stall doors in the bathrooms, because you worried there was always somebody listening. I don't want to be in that position."

Scott had his own frustrations. "It's been two-and-a-half years since John's death, and because the trial hasn't even started yet, it's like it flashes in front of your face all the time when you least expect it. You'll be watching the news and they'll say, 'Colorado started picking jurors for the trial,' and you're saying, 'Oh my God, I got a four-month trial I'm still facing.' That kind of dredges it all back up."

"It" all began sometime before 1 a.m. at the Century 16 theater in Aurora, a town of 339,000 people, roughly ten miles outside of Denver. Witnesses described a lone gunman dressed in black ballistic armor and wearing a mask, who opened fire at a crowded midnight screening of the new Batman movie, *The Dark Knight Rises.*

Police said the shooter paid for his ticket before taking a seat in the front row of theater nine; twenty minutes into the film, he left the building from the emergency exit door, propping it open with a plastic tablecloth holder. He returned wearing combat gear and carrying weapons and tear gas, which witnesses said he threw into the crowd.

"Every few seconds, it was just boom, boom, boom," a movie-goer would later tell CNN. "He would reload and shoot, and any-one who would try to leave would just get killed."

Hundreds of calls from people inside the theater flooded 911. Police arrived at the scene about 12:40 a.m., within a minute and a half of the first call for help. It was mayhem: Dozens of people were running out of theater nine. A total of seventy-one people were either shot or injured in the attack; ten people died at the scene, and two others died from their wounds on the way to the hospital. Police immediately detained Holmes, who was found just standing near his white car with an AR-15 assault rifle, a Remington 870 twelve-gauge shotgun, and a .40-caliber Glock handgun; another handgun was in the car.

Within a few hours, two hundred police officers were at the scene, interviewing witnesses and searching the large parking lot for any additional evidence they could find.

But police were in for another big surprise: when Holmes was apprehended, he told officers he had booby-trapped his apart-ment with incendiary and chemical devices, forcing authorities to evacuate five nearby buildings. Tenants of the building wouldn't be allowed to return to their homes for nearly six days.

Kathleen and Scott had no idea that tragedy had struck in the early morning hours, until one of their daughters called them at 7:15 a.m.

"She said, 'Have you seen the news?' and we said, 'No, what happened?'" recalled Kathleen. "She told us what the news was reporting."

They were not the only ones caught off guard. By the time the shooting began, newsrooms across the country were already empty. There was only one person left at *The Denver Post*, the largest publication in Colorado.

As the nation awoke hours later, major websites and cable and television networks were retelling the horrific details of what had transpired at the multiplex theater in Aurora, based not on traditional reporting—there hadn't been time to do any yet—but on real-time, first-hand accounts posted on Twitter and other social media.

Through Facebook, the Larimers discovered that John had gone to the movie theater with a few Navy buddies and a woman he had started dating a few weeks earlier.

"So all of us tried calling him and we were texting him, but we didn't know if he was at work or what," Kathleen said. "We didn't know what was going on. The police were not much help, they just said call the hospital." But the hospital didn't have anything to tell them either.

Questions ping-ponged between them: Did he get shot? What did the military know? If he had been shot, why hadn't he been identified? Where was his wallet and ID? All the family could really do was sit and wait for answers.

It wasn't long before the unknown killer had an identity and a face. His wild-eyed expression and flaming red hair showed up on television screens, the internet, and in print, prompting concern that hyperventilating coverage of the killer might inspire copycats. (Time would prove the critics right. Just five months later, an even deadlier mass shooting occurred, this time at Sandy Hook Elementary in Newtown, Connecticut. Police investigators would later reveal the young killer, Adam Lanza, was obsessed with earlier mass tragedies, including Columbine in 1999, Aurora, and two others discussed in this book: the DC Sniper shootings in 2002 and the Amish school shooting in Pennsylvania in 2006.)

But, at the time, news editors covering the Aurora shooting were concerned with a more immediate problem: the early morning hours of the tragedy left them without the usual reporting on the victims and the emotional journeys of worried families. Reporters were quickly dispatched to Colorado and other parts of the country where they could find relatives of the dead victims, such as the Larimers, who were all gathered at Kathleen and Scott's home in Illinois.

By mid-afternoon the Larimers still hadn't heard from John, but they were sure he had gone to the theater. Kathleen and Scott decided they needed to call their relatives in order to warn them that John might have been one of the victims in the Aurora massacre.

"We called my mother and my sister," said Kathleen. "And Scott called his sister, and our kids started letting their in-laws know."

What they didn't expect was that those calls, somehow, would ultimately lead to media trucks rolling onto their quiet neighborhood streets, their lives from then on inundated with reporters.

The first call came in at 3:30 p.m.

"We were waiting to hear about John when all of a sudden the phone rang; it was this reporter who started asking questions. I'm like, 'How did they figure this out? I don't want to talk to them. I don't want to talk to anybody,'" Kathleen remembered. "We didn't know what happened to John yet. We were fearing the worst but at the same time we didn't know."

When the reporter posted online what little information he managed to get out of them, the media arrived within an hour.

It was the last thing the Larimers needed. "I looked at it like this," said Kathleen. "I didn't want to deal with them. Why were they here? Initially we were waiting and hoping that John was going to be okay and then it's like, now we have them on our doorstep asking questions that we don't want to answer. It was more of an annoyance."

Television crews parked large satellite trucks on one side of the street, as print reporters arrived with their notebooks, cell phones, and endless curiosity. Within a short time, the media pack grew to at least thirty people.

"The press came down on our house like flies in the night, right after it got leaked out that John might have been one of people killed," Scott said.

"First it was that he was missing," corrected Kathleen. "We weren't sure that he was one of the dead. The law enforcement in Colorado took so long in releasing the names of those who were found on the floor of the theater."

The Larimers put a cloth over the door facing the street, hoping to keep reporters from looking in. But inside the home, the phone never stopped ringing.

"It was the media, one after the other," Kathleen said.

"Luckily, we had two phone lines at the time," said Kathleen. "So we called family members and said, 'Use our second number,' because we quit answering our primary house number; the calls became too much."

The Larimers also decided there would be no family spokesperson; in fact, there would be no speaking to the media at all. "None of us wanted to be crying on the news," Kathleen said.

And yet, for anyone tuned into the news or reading stories online, it was like watching a timeline of the Larimer's unfolding grief.

"Tonight we await word on the fate of a Crystal Lake native who was inside the theater during the massacre," an NBC-5 Chicago television anchor announced. "The family of John Thomas Larimer spent the day frantically calling Colorado authorities trying to find out what happened to their son."

The anchor tosses the story to a reporter at "the scene"—the scene being the Larimers' neighborhood. The reporter goes on to tell viewers that friends and relatives of the family have been stopping by all night to visit the Larimers, who have politely declined to speak to the media. "Members [of the media] have gone to the door over and over, as they wait for news."

The screen switches to footage outside John's high-school building, where flags are flying half-mast. John's yearbook photograph flashes across the screen. Friends and neighbors are interviewed, describing him as "bright" and "grounded."

"I can't imagine the grief," one neighbor says, holding back tears.

At home, the family still didn't have answers.

"The hospital kept on saying that they didn't have anybody unidentified," recalled Kathleen. "So as the day went on, we were more and more sure that one of the people lying on the floor was John, but how was it that he had not yet been identified?"

By 8:15 p.m., they'd received word that John was dead.

"We actually received two notifications," Scott said.

The first came from one of their sons, who flew to Colorado to try to get some answers. "The police told him that John was on the casualty list, and then a couple of hours later, at midnight, the Navy notification team showed up at our door. But by that time we already had the bad news."

Even more attention was directed at the Larimer family once Julia Vojtsek, the woman who was with John at the theater, provided the *Chicago Sun Times* with a statement about their last moments. Then, John's portrayal in the media went from "bright" and "grounded" to "hero."

"John and I were seated in the middle area. When the violence occurred, John shielded me from a spray of gunshots," Julia wrote, shortly after John's death made headlines. "It was then I believe John was hit with a bullet that would have very possibly struck me. I feel very strongly I was saved by John, who immediately and instinctively covered me and brought me to the ground in order to protect me from danger."

The Denver Post wrote, "John Thomas Larimer's last act was a heroic act. It was not, however, an act of bravery performed in his role as a Navy sailor—it was an act of love and sacrifice performed as a boyfriend."

That first night, the press packed up and left before 10:30 p.m., but they were back the next morning.

"We must have had six or eight newspapers and TV stations camped outside our door, from first sun to dark," Scott said. "The police came by and told us if they got to be too obnoxious to let them know and they would make sure the media followed the ordinance of Crystal Lake so they would not be intrusive."

Scott never considered calling the police on the reporters. "They were never disrespectful. They were across the street with all their cameras and telescopic lenses. You can find pictures of us when the Navy notification team came again to the house as we were leaving to go to the funeral home. The media took pictures of that, too."

Scott shared a story about the military motorcade that brought his son's body to the funeral home: Scott and Kathleen's grandchildren were able to watch the dramatic scene, which lasted forty minutes, on TV, since the media was providing live coverage from two news helicopters hovering from above.

"Literally every police station, every fire station, every library, most of the intersections had people lined up shoulder to shoulder, waving flags or with their hands over their hearts," he said. "It's all on Google," he added.

He was right. It was all on Google, which led me to wonder out loud: Did Kathleen and Scott feel like their privacy was invaded, since we now all had access to their private grief?

"They took pictures of our house from across the street. They took pictures of us when we left for the funeral home to make John's burial arrangement," Scott said. "But when we said no, they took no as an answer. They have a job to do, and I respect that, that's their livelihood. I can't recall any time that the media was nasty, mean, or intrusive, or anything but very respectful."

I could tell Scott was trying to find a way for me to see exactly what he meant.

"You know how you see those candlelight vigils on television and people are standing around waiting for somebody to say something, that's basically the way that it was."

Kathleen had her own thoughts. "I was discussing this with one of my daughters. And she said every time she went outside, she was questioned. And I wondered if some of it is an age thing too? We were a little older, and are John's parents. I wondered if the media handled us more carefully than they handled John's older sister. She felt when she walked outside she got peppered with questions."

I wondered, too, but had no answer. In my family's experience, age didn't seem to matter; we always had a mic or a camera on us, just waiting.

I reminded them of what they had told me earlier—that they rarely talked to reporters. Could that have kept the media at arm's length?

Scott's voice rose with excitement. "I think that's probably the number-one thing, if there's a lesson learned. I'm not exactly an experienced person with the media, but I think it's like feeding a stray dog, and I'm not saying the press is like a stray dog, but if you feed it once, it will be back looking for more."

But could there be something else, too? The Larimers were a big, close-knit family, who not only had the support of a huge list of relatives, but were well liked in the community where they had lived for nearly four decades and were part of the large military family, who saw John's death as a loss of one of their own. All of these things helped them stay insulated from the media.

Shirley Wygal, whose thirty-two-year-old daughter Rebecca was also killed in the theater, did not have the support the Larimers had; in fact, she felt utterly alone. Less than a year earlier, she had moved to Colorado to be with Rebecca and with her two grandchildren.

"Any other time, if there had been an emergency situation I would have called Rebecca. That would have been the first thing I did and I would have bounced things off of her, regarding what should I do and how I should handle a situation. We were really good for each other in that way."

But Rebecca had vanished, and Shirley had only herself to rely on. "My two sons were on the road headed to Colorado from Texas. They were getting their information piecemeal, like I was."

When she pulled into the Aurora police station that afternoon, still just hours after the shooting, to try to get more information from the authorities, she noticed a media crew was also in the parking lot. "The guy from the press just walked up and started talking to me," she said. "I didn't know the media were not really our friends. I didn't realize that, but I learned later."

She didn't have any details of what happened at the theater until just before she spoke to the reporter in the parking lot. "I had received a phone call from my son. He told me he'd been told there was a shooting at a theater and the last time Rebecca was seen, she was on the ground, and breathing. I knew something happened, and I knew no one could find Rebecca. But I sure didn't know she had been shot. I was about to walk into the police station. I wanted to know if there was a Jane Doe. That's when the reporter said, 'I can find out for you.' He had someone call the police station. And he came back and said, 'Yes, a Jane Doe is at the University of Colorado Hospital.'"

News footage of that day shows Shirley looking worried but brave, nervously holding her temples as she listens to someone on the other end of her cell phone.

"I think it's serious," she says to the person on the other end.

On air, the reporter explains how they found Shirley in the parking lot of the Aurora police department after she had been frantically going from one hospital to another in search of her daughter, Rebecca Wingo.

While I watched the footage of her from that day, I thought I heard a hint of hope in her voice, as if she believed her daughter was still alive.

"Yes. At that point, that's absolutely what I was thinking. I still didn't know for sure she had gone to the theater."

The cameras show Shirley driving off in her car to the hospital, but before that moment, when the camera wasn't rolling, she gave the crew a photograph of Rebecca wearing a yellow shirt, as well as her cell phone number, which ultimately was shared with other reporters.

"At the time, it was fine with me because I had been asking people to help me find her and I wanted them to know who to look for."

Later in the week, the news station ran another interview. A reporter speaks in voice-over, reminding viewers about the first time they met Shirley, on Friday. Again, they show footage of her driving out of the parking lot that day. The reporter's voice quickly turns somber, as he explains that later that day Shirley realized Rebecca was dead.

"My goal in talking to the media again was to correct the errors that were being made. Reporting that Rebecca was just a single mother of two working at the Crab Shack is not an accurate description of my daughter. I wanted to make sure that everybody knew she had an incredible mind and an amazing spirit. She was a veteran of the United States Air Force and had been a Mandarin Chinese linguist for them for ten years. She had been going to community college, to realize her dream of becoming a social worker. She had just landed a full-time job with a big company and was raising two beautiful daughters. I was not going to let them recreate history."

I wondered, how did she feel now, two years later, about that moment in the parking lot? "At the time, the last thing I was thinking was that these people were not on my side or that they would exploit me or that I was vulnerable. None of that entered my thinking."

Since the tragedy, Shirley had been preparing for the trial and reading up on how other victims of crimes have been treated in various high-profile cases. "Compared to what I've been reading about, I now believe the media treated me very gently. I don't think they ever intruded on my privacy or were hostile."

Still, she had her issues with the media, like when a certain newspaper would not stop publishing a photograph she did not give them permission to use. That same publication, she said, printed information that was incorrect about how her daughter died.

"There are definitely different accounts being told of what happened in the theater that night, regarding Rebecca's death. Some stories are much more reliable than others, and when the evidence is revealed in trial, all the liars will be singled out."

There were other things she wasn't happy about. "In every interview they always ask, 'What else do you want to say?' Well, I wanted to say thank you to people for all the support I had received, but they never reported that. I take issue with these long interviews I would give, and then they pick well-chosen statements that make whatever point *they* were trying to make."

In my mind, Shirley's privacy *was* invaded, and while she was at her most vulnerable, in the parking lot frantically looking for her child. But at that moment, Shirley saw the journalists she spoke to as the only ones with answers to her questions.

I felt similarly about Kathleen and Scott's experience with the media. I was happy their encounters with reporters during the most troubling time in their life had been good ones; they feel that they were treated with the utmost respect. But for me, the scene in front of their home, under siege from reporters and helicopters waiting for them to make any movement, sounds disrespectful and invasive. Even though, as Scott told me, "it's their job."

I worry on behalf of all the families my father and I spoke to about the upcoming trial: Will the media hang back respectfully and give the families space and time to grieve, or will it be too tempting not to take advantage of a situation where all of the victims are in one room?

"It just makes it hard for the healing to start when there's always something going on that brings back this thing, including the trial. I'm kind of dreading the trial, because it's going to be like yanking a scab off of a wound," Scott said.

I understood Scott's point. How is healing possible for the Larimers, and for Shirley, when a trial threatens to reveal details they may not want to hear, and will force them to look in the eyes of the man who brutally killed their loved ones? And then, there is something else to consider: reporters will be sitting shoulder to shoulder beside them in a courtroom, with a camera looming above, watching every move.

Having been subjected to a lack of privacy during my own family's most private moments, I knew the path for the Larimers, Shirley, and the other families like them would be bumpy.

"I'm hoping the media is not going to show up in front of our hotel door, so we don't have to change motels every couple of days and so we don't have to hide out from them," Kathleen said. "I feel better now, because, how it's been described, it won't be like your trial."

Shirley doesn't even know how she's going to afford to *attend* the trial. After her daughter's death, the grandchildren remained with their father in Colorado while Shirley retreated to Texas, where she works as a substitute teacher and struggles to make ends meet.

Her anger, she told me, is the one thing that energizes her.

"Anger keeps me going. I don't know how long one can go on doing that, though. I think I'm wearing myself out. I'm sad."

She also realizes that true healing won't come until the person who killed her daughter is dealt with, even if that means the wounds will remain open a little longer.

"I've come to terms with all the potential outcomes, so I can live with it," she said. "I just want to get there. I want to get to the end. I want to get to thinking about Rebecca and not about her killer. That's what this is about for me."

ESAW AND
EMERALD GARNER

Wife and daughter of police brutality victim Eric Garner

July 17, 2014

Eric and Esaw's daughter Emerald with Eric's mother, Gwen Carr (center), and Esaw, December 2014. (Photo: Andrew Kelly, Reuters)

E saw Garner, the widow of Eric Garner, has not seen the full video of her late husband dying after police in Staten Island, New York, put him into what appeared to be a chokehold on July 17, 2014. In the chilling video, the forty-three-year-old father of six and grandfather of two loses consciousness after telling cops eleven times that he can't breathe.

"I've only seen what the media has shown," Esaw told me. "I haven't seen the entire video. It's bad enough that the last words he spoke are being broadcast all over the place."

Since the video went viral, Esaw has spent most of her time with a camera pointed at her, too. "I haven't even had a chance to mourn yet. Sometimes I sit quietly and I cry, but it's not the same. I'm damn near desensitized to it by now."

Unlike most people I've spoken to for this book, Esaw and her family are still in "the battle," both legally and emotionally—true examples of what it's like for a family suddenly thrust in the "spotlight," as Esaw calls it.

I spoke to her less than three months after the grand jury announced its decision not to indict police Officer Daniel Pantaleo on charges he fatally choked her husband of twenty-five years. The decision came in the wake of a series of unarmed deaths of African-American men in 2014, and only days after a grand jury elected not to charge the police in the death of Michael Brown, a teen fatally shot by a police officer in Ferguson, Missouri.

When we talked, it was just eight months after her husband's death, and Esaw was still raw, teetering between the strong spitfire woman born and bred in Brooklyn and the distraught, broken-hearted wife.

Like most of us, forty-six-year-old Esaw is not used to being in front of the media. She doesn't come off as a "perfect" victim on television, though she does seem natural, strong, and brutally honest.

"I don't care about what people say about me, because they don't know me."

Gwen Carr, Eric's mother, is better in front of the camera, Esaw confesses, which is why she has decided to let her mother-in-law start taking over public speaking. "I'm done."

What I loved about my conversation with Esaw was how genuine she is. She speaks off the cuff, and her emotions are all over the place, but she never puts on airs.

There's a roughness about her; maybe it's just the heavy Brooklyn accent. Or maybe it's the things she says, like "I'm hood."

But her tough way of talking can turn eloquent, almost poetic, on a dime as she discusses her loss and the injustice done to her husband. "When they took away his breath, they took away mine."

But no one can take away who she really is, even if she chooses to rein herself in for the cameras.

To keep from saying the wrong thing or going off in front of media—CNN, *Meet the Press*, MSNBC, the *Daily News*—Esaw told me she created an alter ego, a representative for her dead husband, her children, and grandchildren.

"The person you see in the media, that's not me. That's my CEO, that's Esaw. But I'm really 'Pinky in the Hood.' I keep it real," she told me. "My lawyer tells me, 'Esaw you are so raw.' I have no filter. Sometimes I have to sit and really think *What am I saying?* because I am in the media now and they will twist my words."

I asked her, was it hard to make that transition from ordinary person still in shock and anger, to someone who is in front of the camera all the time?

"Yes! Did you see the interview where they asked if I would accept the police officer's condolences?" She was referring to a reporter who asked whether the family would accept Officer Pantaleo's statement, "It was never my intention to harm anyone."

I told her I did see the news conference.

"You see my daughter grab my hand like, 'Ma, take your hands off your hips'?"

I caught that too.

"They know once I start putting my hands on my hips, it's about to go down. So they were like, 'Mom, calm down.'"

A day prior, on December 3, a grand jury announced its decision not to indict Pantaleo on charges he choked Esaw's husband to death, setting off protests, mostly peaceful ones, from New York City to Oakland, California. Protesters shut down the West Side Highway in New York City as well as the Brooklyn Bridge and the Lincoln Tunnel.

No one was more stunned by the grand jury decision than Esaw. During the televised press conference that followed, Esaw, acting as the family "CEO," looks wary and tired, as you would expect given the situation. Surrounded by her family, her lawyer, and the Reverend Al Sharpton, her voice is on the edge of tears, though she keeps it together, speaking loud and strong: "As long as I have a breath in my body, I will fight the fight to the end. Thank you," she says stepping away.

And then, a reporter asks the question: Would she accept Pantaleo's condolences?

She returns to the microphone, hands on hips. She's "Pinky," now.

"Hell no!" she says, letting the words linger, and leaning forward, staring straight at the reporter, who is never seen on camera. She is visibly upset, but she speaks, as she does, resolutely and without hesitation, without any *uh*'s or *um*'s.

"The time for remorse would have been when my husband was yelling to breathe. That would have been the time for him to show some type of remorse or some type of care for another human being's life, when [Eric] was screaming eleven times that

he can't breathe. So there's nothing him or his prayers or anything else that would make me feel any different. I don't accept
his apology. No, I could care less about his condolences. He's still
working. He's still getting a paycheck. He's still feeding his kids,
and my husband is six feet under. And I'm looking for a way to
feed my kids now."

Sharpton immediately shuts down the press conference, but
Pinky is not finished. She leans toward the microphone again, her
eyes full of sorrow as she says, "Who's going to play Santa Claus for
my grandkids this year?"

The reporter, still unseen, is clearly excited, wanting to keep
the emotions rolling, when he shouts, "So what do you want to
happen to him? What do you want?"

Esaw resumes her CEO role, and doesn't take the bait. Pinky
is on lockdown. She shakes her head and walks off stage with
everyone else.

"Pinky would have went a whole lot further," she tells me. "Al
Sharpton said, 'You know what? That was the perfect response.
You have a right to express your anger. You haven't expressed any
anger since July 17th and that was your one moment to express
your anger and you did it well. Now just lay back and relax. Now
don't give any more angry interviews.'"

Eric and Esaw met when he was seventeen and she was
twenty.

"We met on a thing called the party line. It was a dating service; we didn't have any of that online stuff back then," she told
me. "We started talking more and more, and then we finally met
up. I'm not going to say it was love at first sight, but when we met
the first time, we knew that it was going to lead to more than just
a casual dating thing."

When she introduced him to her nine-month-old daughter,
Shardineé, and saw the way the "gentle giant" and the baby hit it
off, she knew she had found her husband. They were engaged on
August 16, 1989, and married ten days later.

In 2009, they separated for a time, but about eight months before Eric's death, they reconciled. The Garners are a big family: Shardineé is the oldest at twenty-seven; Dorothy, who Esaw was pregnant with when she first met Eric, died in 1997 from a brain aneurysm at the age of nine; together they had Erica, who is now twenty-five; Emerald, twenty-four; Eric Jr., twenty-one; and Emory, their second son and youngest child, fifteen.

At the time of his death, Eric had another baby, a daughter named Legacy, born during the couple's separation.

"We were doing everything we possibly could to be happy with the grandchildren and with the children. We were doing a lot of family things, spending a lot of time together. So for him to go out one day and not come back was a total shock, unwarranted and devastating."

People who knew Eric describe him as "The Big E" and "Teddy Bear" and "the Neighborhood Peacemaker." Ramsey Orta, the twenty-two-year-old man and friend of Eric's who filmed Eric's death, calls him the "father of the neighborhood."

Esaw said her husband loved nothing better than to treat his family to dinner at his two favorite restaurants: Red Lobster and Junior's in Brooklyn. "He was all about doing things outside the norm. Like getting out of the hood and doing something different."

Esaw and I spoke the day after Valentine's Day. Her voice trembled a little as she offered me some insight into the romantic side of her "Boo."

"My friends used to say, 'Wow, after fifteen years of marriage you still get flowers?' He was always buying me flowers and candy and had Edible Arrangements delivered to my job. It would just be a regular day and I would answer the door and there it would be, and he'd say, 'Babe, did you get your package?' and I would be like, 'Yeah, what's that for?' He'd say, 'Just to let you know that you are my everything,' and I say, 'Aw, Boo, that's sweet.' He liked to romance you . . . He liked to take you out and dress up and go out."

The morning of July 17, Eric was sneezing horribly. His asthma had forced him years earlier to quit a job as a horticulturist at the New York City Department of Recreation. That morning the sneezing caught Esaw's attention.

"I'm like, 'Babe, you alright?' and he said, 'I'm okay. I just need my sinus medicine.' I said, 'Don't you think you should stay in the house today?' and he said, 'No, babe, I got bills to pay. I got things to do. I can't make money sitting in the house.'"

About 11:30 a.m., he kissed her goodbye. Three hours later he send her a text: *Baby, I'm good.*

But when one of their sons returned home with distressing news, she worried he wasn't so good after all.

"He said, 'Ma, somebody just said that the cops choked Daddy out on Bay Street.'" Esaw, not comprehending what her eldest son was saying, assumed her husband was at the police precinct, so she planned to call there and then head over.

Esaw said her husband had a strained relationship with the police, though she said he never resisted arrest. He believed he had been repeatedly harassed by officers. It has been widely reported that Eric had many run-ins with law since the eighties, including driving without a license, marijuana possession, false impersonation, and the more recent accusations that he was selling "loosies," untaxed cigarettes, which is a misdemeanor in New York City. A recent story in the *New York Times,* published after Eric's death, reported that he had made an official handwritten complaint in federal court after an officer allegedly performed a public cavity search on him in 2007. *The New York Times* story also said that, more recently, Eric told Legal Aid he planned to take the cases against him to trial.

"The police thought he was a nuisance," Esaw said.

Despite her son's information and the choking rumor, Esaw did not think there was anything dire going on—that is, until her phone began ringing nonstop. "I'm in a fog almost. The phone calls are just coming through to my phone, before I could even call for the cab to go down to the police station."

Esaw was completely in the dark about what transpired on Bay Street, but thanks to Orta having recorded it all with his cell phone, she soon found out. Sometime before 4:45 p.m., Orta and Eric were on their way to get something to eat, but their plans were interrupted when a fight broke out nearby. According to Orta, Eric broke up the fight. When the police arrived, Orta later told reporters, the officers focused only on Eric, accusing him of selling unlicensed cigarettes.

On the video, Eric, who is unarmed, looks every bit his size: six foot three and 350 pounds. He appears obviously frustrated, but what seems just as obvious is that he and the police have been here before. Eric's comments are tinged with familiarity: "Every time you see me, you want to mess with me," and "I'm tired of this. It stops today," and "Please just leave me alone. I told you the last time . . . just leave me alone."

More police arrive, and one officer in particular grabs Eric around the neck, using what appears to be a chokehold, which had been banned by the New York Police Department. In the video, you can see Eric swat his arms, and say, "Don't touch me." Several others pull him to the ground.

An officer appears to be pressing Eric's face to the sidewalk. Orta is heard telling them to give him oxygen. Police and the EMS would later be criticized for not giving him CPR, but both groups say they believed he was still breathing. Eric died an hour later, on his way to the hospital.

Meanwhile, the confused Esaw received a phone call from someone at the scene on Bay Street who told her to head to the hospital. Accompanied by her friend Linda, Esaw told the receptionist her name, and immediately knew something was wrong from the look on the woman's face. "She said, 'Okay, just a second,' and she went to the back and somebody else came out and

said, 'Who are you?' I said, 'I'm his wife.' The person said 'Mrs.
Garner, could you follow me?' They lead me way around to the
back of the hospital to these back rooms and then they put me
in this little room, with just a chair, a desk, and a phone and a
couch. My girlfriend Linda was still with me. She said, 'Pinky,
you alright?' I said, 'No, I feel it. He's gone. He's no longer here.'
She said, 'Stop saying that.'"

More than two hours later, a throng of doctors and medical
workers walked toward her. "Aw shit, here it comes," she whispered to Linda.

One of the doctors asked her to have a seat. "I said, 'No. Whatever it is you need to tell me, just tell me. Standing up or sitting
down, it ain't going to make no difference.' Then they said, 'We
tried and tried but we couldn't save him.' And that's the last thing
I heard them say. I remember my knees buckling and my uncle
holding me up. I remember the doctor asking me if I wanted to
see him. I was just blank. I didn't know if I wanted to see him
like that; I didn't know if I wanted to hug him one last time or
if I wanted to kiss him on the forehead. I didn't know what I
wanted to do."

All she kept thinking about was how she was going to tell her
children.

"So I just started calling them and telling them to come to
Staten Island. And they are saying, 'What happened? What happened?' I'm like, 'Just come to my house,' and I hung up the phone.
And they kept calling me and calling and I wouldn't answer the
phone because I didn't want to tell them over the phone."

Once the medical examiner ruled the death a homicide,
almost a month after Eric died, things turned surreal.

"Right after that came the media," she said.

Actually, the media came much earlier. It only took reporters
a day to find Esaw, and once they did, they did not relent.

"The Friday after he was killed is when the *Daily News* found
out about me. Because they were thinking that the baby mama

seen crying on the street was Eric's wife. I guess somebody on Bay Street must have told them that's not his wife, and that his wife lives on Jersey Street and her name is Pinky. So they came to me that Friday afternoon; they realized he had a wife and the kids."

I was curious how she was treated once reporters connected the dots. After my brother's murder, the media parked outside of our house for weeks; did she experience that as well?

"Yes. Once they knew who I was and where I lived, they were all over me. I couldn't even sit in front of my building and have a conversation with my neighbors."

They camped out in front of her home, just so they could get a glimpse of "Eric's wife."

"They were peeking through the bushes! I had to have the local guys, the ones that stand around the corner all day, chase them out of here. 'Yo, get out of here. Get away from us. She doesn't want to answer no questions.' One of my girlfriends even went as far as to stand in front of me and do a booty dance, to stop them from filming me."

We both chuckled at that.

I shared with her that I had a hard time finding details about her husband's plans to file a lawsuit against the police department for harassment. I asked Esaw if she felt the media coverage was one-sided—if the whole story was being filtered through a biased lens.

"Yes, because the media didn't let me tell them that [about Eric's plans to file the lawsuit]. They didn't let me tell them the stuff I am telling you. They didn't let me say these things. They want it to be racial, because race is a bigger part of it," she said. "It will call attention to other black men being killed and not just his particular case."

Shortly after her husband's death, Esaw left Staten Island and moved to the Chelsea neighborhood on Manhattan's West Side. Fearful something could happen to her two sons, because of who their father was and because she couldn't deny that young, unarmed black men were being killed, she stopped Emory from going out on Halloween, and keeps a tight leash on Eric Jr., who's in college in New Jersey.

"My husband was killed less than three blocks away from where I lived. The precinct is right there." She explained that if she'd stayed in Staten Island and were to call 911 or the police for something, the officers and emergency workers that came to her aid would have been the same ones who were with her husband at the time of his death.

Being away from Staten Island means she doesn't have to worry about the officers—or about reporters hanging outside her door, since they don't know where she lives. But strangers do recognize her.

"I go to the supermarket, and people are like, 'I'm so sorry for your loss.' They give me hugs. The police officers are very nice over here where I'm at in Chelsea. So it's a whole different atmosphere from Staten Island."

A movement was born that day in July 2014. It started a national conversation about race, police brutality, and abuse of power.

Her husband's death and all that followed was one of the biggest news stories of 2014. The video of Eric crying out "I can't breathe" played constantly. "I can't breathe" T-shirts were worn by athletes and musicians. Even President Obama and former President George W. Bush commented on Eric's death.

But was this a good thing for Eric's family?

Did Esaw resent that her life and family were being paraded around at press conferences and marches, television interviews, for others to gawk at, judge, or sympathize with?

"I'm resentful *only* about the funeral, because I felt that I should have had at least an hour or so to spend with my husband before they put him in the ground, and before the media and the public and everybody else came to the funeral. That's the only thing that I feel resentful about."

The funeral was packed, with mourners inside the Brooklyn church and observers outside surrounding it. Cameras flashed as pallbearers carried the large white casket. Video footage of Esaw overcome by grief and her children giving eulogies dominated the internet.

"They cheated me out of grieving for my husband. You don't want to be all distraught and carrying on in front of cameras. You don't want to have a camera in front of your face while you are crying or while you are expressing how you feel with this great loss, because it was a great loss."

But the protesters, especially, helped her stay strong. Shortly after the grand-jury decision, protesters used Twitter and Facebook to organize all over the country. Within a short time after the decision, supporters gathered at New York City's most iconic sites, including Grand Central Station and Times Square.

Esaw even told a story about being awakened by her son one day, shortly after her husband's death, to look out the window of their Staten Island apartment. Hundreds of protesters were chanting her husband's name as they streamed past. The scene brought her to tears. That same week, she was driving in Lower Manhattan when her path was blocked by demonstrators. She was overwhelmed once again, and got out of the car. The protesters told her it was all for her husband. She thanked them as the crowd let her car through.

Although she appreciated all the love and compassion, she knows what is happening is much bigger than her and Eric.

"I didn't want people to scream, 'I can't breathe,' but it really didn't matter what I wanted. But every protest we went to, that is what they were yelling. The first Saturday after Eric passed, Reverend Sharpton gave a rally in Staten Island in a church. As I was walking, they are separating the crowd and people are yelling in support of me, and you could hear them saying, 'I can't breathe.' And I would just collapse. I just couldn't hear it. Every time I would hear it, I would break down; it took until I got to the march in DC [on December 14th], only until that particular day, I accepted the meaning behind 'I can't breathe.'"

Thousands attended that same march in Washington, DC, where Esaw and her family joined relatives of other African-American men shot by police, including Michael Brown; at the same time, similar events were happening on Fifth Avenue in New York City, in Boston, and in San Francisco.

The demonstrators—some reports claimed there were more than 10,000 in attendance—chanted "I can't breathe," but this time Esaw didn't collapse. She was spirited by those words.

"My husband was a quiet man," she told the crowd. "But he's making a lot of noise right now. His voice will be heard."

Later that month, an estimated 25,000 people marched again for Eric, this time in New York City. By the end of December, a total of fifty demonstrations across the country had been held for him, and hundreds of rallies took place, with Eric's death and police brutality against unarmed African-American men as the focus.

Though she hadn't seen the footage, I wondered how Esaw felt about the video of her husband dying airing on the news and on the internet for the whole world to see. Was she able to appreciate the power of Orta's video?

"Yeah, every time I see Orta I give him a hug. I just tell him, 'Thank you. Thank you so much because without you, Eric would not be recognized; he would just be another dead nigger on the street.'"

Esaw is still adjusting to the spotlight the video has shined on her. Being in front of the media is something she is not yet used to. Criticism can be harsh, and words get twisted.

After she was a guest on a news program, she heard comments about the change in her appearance, how she went from a homely-looking woman to a woman with a long, luxurious weave within a day or two.

"First of all, my hair is not a weave. That's number one."

Second, she explained, she looked different because the news show professionally made up her face and styled her hair.

Another time, she said a major television station made her sound as if she had called her husband "lazy."

"They chopped that interview up so bad to where they have people thinking that I said my husband was fat and lazy . . . I never said that," she told me. "I am an honest person. I feel like, I've been married to him for twenty-seven years, and I know him better than his mother knows him. I can say whatever I want to say about my husband. If they don't like it, then too damn bad. He *was* lazy but I didn't say lazy in the sense of the word like he didn't want to work. I meant he preferred staying home with me."

I told her I learned the hard way that everything gets reduced to a sound bite. And I asked, overall, did she feel the media had been kind to her or unfair?

"The *Daily News* has been wonderful. They will not bother me unless they ask first. There's one person from the *Daily News* that I gave my number to. He'll call me occasionally when something happens in the news. He'll call me and ask me for a comment and I'll tell him no comment because I'll be making a statement Saturday at the National Action Network. And that's that. He doesn't bother me anymore."

Despite all the frustration she has gone through, Esaw believes the reporters are only doing their jobs. "I guess they have to separate their emotions from their job. They can't feel what I feel, doing the job that they're doing . . . I don't think the media's bad. They haven't done anything to me personally to make me feel like they are."

She doesn't think all cops are bad either. "I'm not anti-police. I do have respect for police officers who respect me, and respect their uniform. You put on that uniform to protect and serve, not to execute at your will."

I, too, have tremendous respect for law enforcement, despite how things fared in my brother and Nicole's murder trial, because for me, they were the only ones fighting for Ron, when he couldn't fight for himself.

So when the police are under scrutiny, my first reaction is to defend their honor. I struggle when I hear and see stories about "excessive force" and "abuse of power." It angers me because I don't want to believe that people we trust to protect us could harm us too.

So when these cases flood the airwaves, and the momentum carries from the internet to the street, it pains my heart, because I see a system breaking down even more. The public becomes suspicious of all police; people's faith and trust become compromised when bad apples spoil the bushel. But is that reaction, perhaps, unwarranted?

To Esaw, her husband's *death* was unwarranted. Nothing will change that. But her heart lifts every time she sees just how his death has helped, encouraged, and inspired so many people, including her own children.

Her daughter Emerald has become an outspoken young leader, speaking at marches alongside her mother and grandmother. She's often photographed attending protests and quoted in blogs. In December 2014, newspapers and television news shows showed Emerald laying a wreath at the makeshift memorial for two police officers who were gunned down in New York City days earlier. "I don't want anybody else to feel the hurt that I felt," she told me in a separate conversation. "I don't want no one else to cry as much as I've cried."

Being in the public eye hasn't been easy for Emerald, either. "It's a lot of pressure because you have to watch what you say and watch what you do; it's not a good feeling to know that eyes are on you."

But she told me she understands she can help other young people going through hard times, too.

"I've been in a situation where a total stranger came up to me and said, 'I lost a parent just like you and I was quiet about it, but

I feel like I want to talk about it now.' It's kind of weird but at the same time I'm like, 'I got it. I understand now. I understand my role.'"

As for Esaw, she knows it is too early for her own healing to begin. The pain, the anger, and the hurt are still there. "I feel like my future is at a standstill. They killed my husband. I have no future. I have a future as far as finish raising my [youngest] son and helping my daughters with my grandkids, but as far as where I am, I'm left now without a husband."

I understood how Esaw felt. But she has been brave during such extreme circumstances. "You and your family have done some incredible things with peace rallies and marches," I told her. "Do you feel like that's your future now? Is that your platform now, to be an advocate and lobby for change?"

Esaw seemed to brighten up. "My husband would say, 'Til death do us part and even after.' It meant that even if one of us dies, the other one will still be tied to that one. He made a way for me to be busy and not have time for a relationship. He doesn't want me to be with anybody else."

TERE DUPERRAULT FASSBENDER

Survivor of family's
brutal murder at sea

November 12, 1961

Top left: The Dupperault family together in Wisconsin, 1956. From left to right: Tere (then Terry Jo), Arthur, Jean, Rene, and Brian. *Top Right:* Tere (in hat) with her siblings Rene and Brian. *Center left:* Tere and her brother Brian (both shown here) loved playing survival games in the woods. *Center right:* Tere with her dog Angel, circa 2007. *Bottom:* Tere with her husband, Ron Fassenbender, and her children and grandchildren in their Wisconsin home.

Maybe you've heard the tragic mystery of the Duperraults: a prominent Wisconsin doctor and his picture-perfect family who all vanished on the doomed sixty-foot ketch named *Bluebelle*.

If you were an adult or an adolescent back in the early 1960s, you may remember pieces of the terrifying puzzle: A missing boat. The captain, rescued one day after the ship went down, alongside a dead little girl. The sea of lies he told of his boat catching fire and his attempts to save the ill-fated family.

And, days after the captain's rescue, a beautiful eleven-year-old blonde girl, Terry Jo, the Duperraults' middle child, found drifting alone in the ocean.

Though it was an immediate hot topic, the story and the media spotlight quickly dimmed, for reasons that seem inconceivable today.

The story was told to me by Terry Jo herself, now a sixty-five-year-old grandmother known as Tere Duperrault Fassbender.

In mid-November of 1961, over four horrific days and three merciless nights, Tere had miraculously survived, afloat on a life raft, the blazing sun and the bone-chilling cold of the Atlantic Ocean.

After she realized that her family was dead and the captain had abandoned her, just before *Bluebelle* submerged into the ocean, Tere jumped overboard. There was no food, no water to drink during her days adrift, and she carried with her the horrifying secret of a murderous rampage by a charming killer.

When she was finally rescued by the crew of a passing Greek freighter, dehydrated, in shock, close to death, floating on the Northwest Providence Channel in the Bahamas, she only had the strength to give them a thumbs-down, to indicate no one else on the ship was left. A photograph taken of her sitting in the raft, feet dangling over the sides and looking up, quickly was transmitted around the world, landing her on the cover of *Life* magazine. For a brief period in time, it made her "the most famous girl in world." She even received a note from President Kennedy and a rosary from Pope St. John XXIII.

Then, after six months, the press went radio silent. It wasn't for a lack of interest from the public or the media; rather it was that word had spread among reporters that Tere's well-meaning relatives, the loving aunt and uncle who eventually adopted her, had told family and friends to pretend "it" didn't happen. Journalists back then tended to abide by relatives' requests. And no one kept close-mouthed better than people who knew the Duperraults best, back in Wisconsin: neither her relatives, teachers, best friends, nor even her classmates talked to Tere about what had happened on the high seas.

"It was the big white elephant in the room," Tere told me. "It was uncomfortable for a long time, because no one was allowed to say anything; they treated me fine and normal, but I knew they knew."

She learned to live with staying quiet, but not being able to talk about "it" delayed her healing by decades. It would take her almost twenty years to discuss the tragedy with a psychologist and fifty years to tell the public exactly what happened.

After talking to Tere for nearly two hours, my brain was flooded with complex emotions; there were so many questions I still wanted to ask, and so many lingering what-ifs. What if, for example, instead of growing up a child of the sixties, she were raised in today's Information Age? No doubt, her face would have been plastered on every blog, website, newspaper, magazine, and local and national news channel. Would being so public have been better for her than the media blackout she experienced? Did fifty years of silence help her, or hurt her?

After the *Bluebelle* massacre, Tere was loved and supported by the family members who took her in, but she was also sheltered and isolated. How could she heal, when she couldn't talk about what happened to her and her entire family?

The horrific events of that fateful 1961 voyage started as a beautiful gesture from a hardworking father who had recently been preoccupied with his growing optometry business. All he wanted was to spend time with his children and wife. So Dr. Arthur Duperrault, a World War II US Navy veteran who believed travel was the best educator, dreamed up a family vacation on the high seas, a week of fun off the coast of Florida.

"He would take us to special places, up in Northern Wisconsin, or on the weekends, we'd go swimming to the beach. It was just a real ideal childhood," Tere said.

Living near the countryside, Tere would spend hours playing survival games in the woods, by herself, which would turn out to be just the preparation she'd need for the days spent alone at sea.

"I was just a country girl, loved to be outside. I was pretty much a loner; I spent a lot of time with nature, in the forest. We lived in the country, so you didn't have somebody next door to play with all the time."

But Tere did love to play with her brother Brian, who was three years older. They would go off in the woods, exploring caves, picking grapes. "My brother was this mad chemist; he'd make grape wine out of the grapes we picked and, of course, it blew up in our basement. He was always doing that kind of stuff with chemistry sets, blowing stuff up."

While Brian and Tere were blonds, their younger sister Rene was a spitfire brunette and reminded Tere of their mother, whom Tere describes as a nonconformer.

"My mother was a very different type of person for that time. She was really big into golf, was an artist, and played bridge. I remember her, but I remember my father more. I guess I was like his little girl and I had a special thing for him."

I asked Tere if the memories of her childhood were her own, or those told to her by extended family. I wondered, did she even know the difference anymore?

"I don't have a lot of memories, but the ones I do have are mine. The family members wouldn't have known those things because we lived out in the country. When Brian and I were roaming around the countryside, they wouldn't have known that."

Their exciting trip to the Caribbean was to be a test run, she told me, to see if they had it in them to spend a year traveling around the world on a boat. That was her father's ultimate goal.

Dr. Duperrault chartered the *Bluebelle* for their dream voyage and hired Captain Julian Harvey, a forty-four-year-old World War II hero, and former model, to steer them through the Caribbean. Harvey brought with him Mary Dene, his sixth wife, a former TWA flight attendant who cooked all the meals on board.

"It seemed like everyone got along," Tere said. "I've been asked numerous times about Captain Harvey and his wife. Everything appeared friendly and nice."

That is, until about 9 p.m. on November 12, four days into the trip, when Tere heard her fourteen-year-old brother screaming for their father: "Help, Daddy! Help!"

"Right now, just sitting here, I can see myself. I was lying in this dark cabin when I heard my brother screaming, then I heard some pounding noises. I was waiting to see what was happening. I knew by the sound of my brother's voice that something bad happened. It put me into that place, where you're outside of your body."

When Tere crept, terrified, outside her cabin, she saw her mother and brother lying in a pool of blood. Stricken with fear, she walked slowly, in a dreamlike state, up the stairs and noticed blood spilled on top of the deck and in the back of the cockpit area.

"I saw the captain. I said, 'What's going on? What's happened?' And he came rushing toward me and pushed me. 'You get down there!' And so I went back down. I stayed in my bunker and I waited and I waited and then at some point he came in and opened my door."

Tere trembled, but said not a word to Captain Harvey who stood at the door, staring at her, with what she believes was a rifle in his hand.

"Then he just backed out. At that point water was coming into my bunker and the mattress started floating. I realized that I had to get out of there because the boat was sinking."

She left the cabin, and ran to the upper deck. She saw the dinghy and a rubber raft floating in the water, beside the ship. She shouted to Harvey, "Is the boat sinking?"

"Yes!" he yelled back, and then threw her a line to the dinghy.

She missed it. He rushed toward her—she later believed he was about to kill her—but he turned on his heels once he noticed she had dropped the boat's line, and that now his raft, his only chance at survival, was floating away.

"He dove overboard, to get the dinghy. I watched him swim towards it and then he disappeared."

Abandoned by the captain, on a ship that was going down fast, she realized she had to save herself.

"I remembered where that cork raft was and I went there. During the entire time, it was like I was standing there watching myself do all of this; I got the raft, threw it into the ocean, and jumped in."

She huddled in the little cork raft, worried only about seeing the captain again. "I didn't want to move; I didn't want anyone to see me. I didn't want *him* to see me. So that's what I did all through the night, until daylight came. I didn't move. When daylight came, I could search the horizon and I could see that he wasn't in sight. I was no longer afraid."

But by now, she was in a complete state of shock.

"One day, and it was the worst day, because it was overcast and the waves were just huge, twenty feet, and I was on this little raft, just going with the waves, just miserably cold. And I looked to my side and there I was, in a pod of whales. . . . It gave me peace to know that they were there. It made me feel good and I said to them, 'You're protecting me and it makes me feel really good that you're here.'"

She later mentioned this memory to the US Coast Guards, who said, "No, those were sharks."

Tere told me she knew they were not sharks. "I knew they were whales, pilot whales. But I never argued." To this day, Tere believes the whales were guardians.

My first thought was that it sounded like a naïve thing to say; there she was in the middle of whales or sharks, and she believed— still believes—they were there to protect her? But as I reflected back on her story, her thinking made more sense. Growing up so sheltered, Tere likely expected to be protected—even if that protection came in the form of large, wild sea animals. I wondered if that innocent way of thinking had helped her keep her faith when she was floating aimlessly alone in the middle of the sea.

"I think it could have been innocence," she told me. "But I did have a strong belief in God."

A day after *Bluebelle* went down, while Tere was still lost at sea, Captain Julian Harvey was rescued in the dinghy; beside him was a small rubber raft which carried Tere's seven-year old sister Rene's dead body. A 1962 Coast Guard report stated that the young girl probably drowned after the Captain's rampage. Harvey likely brought her body along to make himself look more credible. (The other bodies were never recovered.)

Two days after he was rescued, and four days past the tragedy, Captain Harvey sat in a hearing room in Miami, spinning a tall tale to the US Coast Guards who were interviewing him about "the accident." He told them the *Bluebelle* caught fire, killing everyone onboard, including his own wife.

The Coast Guard hadn't yet been able to find Tere because the pale-colored clothes she was wearing, her blonde hair, and the white raft, only two-by-five feet long, were all camouflaged by the white caps of the ocean waves. She was impossible to detect, even by helicopters, who flew right past her; Tere's experience is why the Coast Guard officially changed flotation devices to bright international orange, in order to increase visibility against the dark ocean.

By chance, she was finally spotted floating off the coast of the Bahamas by the crew of a Greek freighter, and rescued at just about the same time Captain Harvey was completing the official inquiry.

"They were telling me not to jump out of the raft," she recalled. "I guess because my legs were hanging over, they kept saying, 'Don't jump out.'"

She didn't realize it at the time, but the captain of the ship did not want her to jump because he could see what looked like sharks swimming around the lifeboat.

"I wasn't about to jump, because I saw the crew building a raft to get me. I floated right to them. They said, 'Can you stand up?' and I said, 'Yes,' and then I collapsed and went into a coma."

Back in Miami, a Coast Guard official rushed into the room where Captain Harvey was finishing his interviews, carrying the most remarkable news: Another survivor had been found, a little blonde-haired girl named Terry Jo. Shocked and nervous, the captain leaned back, stood up, and said, "Oh my God!" He quickly excused himself, checked into a hotel, and savagely and fatally slit his own wrist, thigh, and throat.

Tere's rescue at sea, and the captain's suicide, sent the media into a frenzy. Everyone wanted to talk to or see the little lone survivor.

During her stay in the hospital, Tere was all smiles and politeness, but full of worries inside. How would she get back to Green Bay? How would she pay for food? How would she pay for the hospital bill? Was her dad, whose body she hadn't seen on the boat, really dead?

She answered the Coast Guard's every question, but she never mentioned her dead family to the investigators or the hospital workers. The medical staff would later say it was heartbreaking for them to watch, as they realized she was only trying to be "Brave Terry Jo," as she was often called.

The Coast Guard officials were the only ones allowed to question her, and soon after talking to her, they began to rethink Harvey's story. The girl's recollection of events, especially paired with Harvey's suicide, raised serious suspicions about the captain's account of the days prior.

Stringing the facts together, officials theorized that Dr. Duperrault had walked in on Captain Harvey in the act of killing his wife, on whom he had recently taken out an insurance policy. Some people looking into the mystery, including Tere, believe that the only reason Harvey didn't kill Tere was because he figured she'd go down with the ship.

Authorities would later learn that two of Harvey's previous wives died in suspicious accidents; this information about the captain's previous life just added to the drama. The new details continued to pique the media's interest in the lone survivor—the only person who could unlock the mystery.

While reporters' behavior was tame compared to today's media circus, Tere told me they were relentless in Miami, where she was in the hospital; she remembered a reporter who disguised himself as an orderly and tried to get into her room. Luckily, guards stood outside her door at all times, and he was unsuccessful.

When Tere moved back to Wisconsin to live with her aunt and uncle, their sons, and her grandmother, she had no idea of the drama unfolding around her because her family ultimately decided to shield her from it all.

"My family was very protective. But shortly after I returned home, they figured they had to do something with the media, because they had been so respectful. So my aunt and uncle allowed them to come and film me one day, but the reporters weren't allowed to ask any questions. The newspaper was satisfied and they didn't bug me after that."

With no access to her, the media quickly disappeared. People stopped talking about what happened all together. Everyone, including Tere, pretended it didn't happen.

Being in Wisconsin gave Tere the fresh start she sorely needed. Her aunt and uncle sent her to a new school in a nearby town, but everyone still knew who she was. "It was like the minute I walked in, I knew everybody was staring at me. I knew they all knew, and it was just really, really uncomfortable. It was uncomfortable for a long time that way because no one would say anything."

Throughout her teen years she kept being "Brave Terry Jo," but inside she was struggling. "Part of it was, I always believed my father was alive somewhere on some island and I would find him and he would find me. I believed that, because I saw my mother and brother were dead, but because I hadn't seen my father, I thought that he was fine. I just believed in that. I had a lot of trouble through my teen years emotionally not accepting that, even though I was told from the get-go by my attorney that, 'Your father is not alive. You just have to accept it.' I never did inside."

Though she loved her new immediate family, she became closest to her grandmother. "My grandmother was a big part of my life. She lived with us. She listened to me. We read together, we knitted together. She was my rock. My aunt was very overprotective, but I resented that because the boys—my cousins—could do more. They got to go out and I couldn't do that. They had resentment toward me too. I had a trust fund, so I had a car, and everything I needed and wanted."

By the time she was around thirteen, she was sick and tired of being called "Brave Terry Jo," so she changed her name to Tere. "Even to this day when someone calls me Terry Jo, I know they are from my old life."

But changing her name didn't alter what happened and didn't allow her to sidestep the grieving process she was working so hard to avoid.

"Of course, I had been seeing psychiatrists most of my life. When I was younger, I thought, 'La-di-dah-dah. You aren't going to get anything out of me.' I had that kind of attitude, and so it just took me a long time."

I asked her if she was ever angry at the captain, the man who killed her entire family.

She answered, "No."

I raised an eyebrow at her reply, surprised.

Was she was still trying to be "Brave Terry Jo"? Or was she just staying slightly detached as her way of coping?

Living in Green Bay in the sixties, when post-traumatic stress disorder wasn't on anyone's radar and there was only one psychologist in town, she couldn't have had many choices as to how to put back together the pieces of her fractured life. Many people of that generation believed that protecting a child from thinking about bad things was a far better option than talking about them.

"I always referred to my incident as 'the accident' for years and years and years," she told me. "And I never believed Captain Harvey was guilty for years either."

"But he pointed a gun at you," I said to Tere. "You saw your mother and brother dead, lying in a pool of blood. You heard your brother yelling for help!"

"I was always raised not to be judgmental. And if you didn't see it happen, how could you prove it happened? For many, many years, I never held any grudge towards him."

I told Tere that while I'm no psychologist, I have dealt with my share of survivor's guilt, wishing I could have done something to save my brother's life and resenting that I was left to deal with all the pain and anguish that followed his murder.

I wondered if she thought she had subconsciously convinced herself that what happened on the boat was an accident to protect herself in some way.

"Maybe that could be," she said. "I don't know if I've had survivor's guilt. I've had times where I feel some guilt, especially involving my mother and brother. I didn't go up and touch them, when I saw them lying there. But something in me knew they were dead. So I think that's just self-preservation. When I waded through the water to get through the cabin and upstairs when the boat was sinking, I was horrified that I was going to bump into their bodies. It was knee deep, but when I came down both times, I don't remember seeing their bodies. I must have blocked that out somehow, because I would have had to pass them."

By the time she was an adult, and still not talking about her family's deaths, she felt directionless and made many bad choices. Still emotionally searching for a father figure, "I got into some bad marriages," Tere said, "and for all the wrong reasons." Those bad decisions, she recalled, were "just steady and constant."

Things started to change in 1979. Tere, now on her second marriage, this time to a soldier, had just arrived in Germany and was setting up medical care for her three children. During the parent-intake interview, the pediatrician scanned the questionnaire she had filled out and asked something she had never been asked before:

"How did your parents die?"

Before she'd finished telling the story, the doctor insisted she talk to a psychologist friend of his, which she agreed to do. For the first time since the loss of her family, she'd speak of the trauma she endured as a little girl.

It was progress, but she was a long way from the finish line.

As time went on, Tere, now married a third time and living back in Wisconsin, started to get more comfortable with her story, so much so that she agreed to talk to a reporter from a local newspaper and to make an appearance on *Oprah*, in 1988, on a show about survivors.

Tere, the "most famous girl in the world," was now merely one of several telling their harrowing stories of survival to the famous talk-show host.

"This one lady on the show with me had been stabbed seventeen times, and I mean it had just happened to her six months earlier! Then there was this other woman that I think her dad murdered her siblings and her mother and molested her—it was terrible. When I appeared on *Oprah*, I thought I was healed. Compared to the other women on the show, I thought I was in much better shape, because it had all just happened to them and my story was so long ago."

She thought that right up until she returned to her home in Wisconsin. "I was miserable, and realized I was stuck in a bad marriage and I wasn't healed." She'd later write in her memoir, *Alone: Orphaned on the Ocean*, that her third husband was a charmer who hid the fact that he was a pedophile not only during their courtship, but during their marriage. He never victimized her own children, but her two daughters frequently shared that he gave them the creeps.

She divorced her third husband, who went to prison for felony child abuse. And although her husband was out of her life, Tere wasn't even close to being done healing.

Therapeutic help came again in 1999, this time from her friend Richard Logan, a psychologist and expert on sole survivors.

Relatives of Mary Dene, Captain Harvey's wife, thought the story of what happened on the *Bluebelle* was too far-fetched and probably constructed by an eleven-year-old's imagination; that had always bothered Tere. "It just crushed me that they thought I was lying," she told me. "So I held that forever."

To help her resolve any doubts about what she had remembered from her childhood tragedy, Logan suggested she take a truth serum, or sodium amytal, to aid in the honest recollection of events and hopefully to mark the beginning of a real healing process. The truth serum proved successful; it gave her the confidence to know that what she remembered *actually* happened. It also allowed her to get angry, and see Harvey for who he really was.

"I didn't really look at him as the murderer of my family and that was the thing that I was dealing with all this time. It got to the point that I finally did realize that he murdered everybody. It *was* murder; it wasn't an accident. That revelation was just part of my process."

Though she had never before seen herself as a survivor in all of the years since the *Bluebelle* massacre, she finally realized she was, and in the truest sense of the word. The captain left her on the boat, expecting the ocean to engulf her, but instead it saved her life and changed her forever.

"I never had fear of the water. Actually, I respect it," she said. "Sometimes when the waves are just right, it takes me to when I was on the ocean back then."

In fact, until she retired in 2001, she had built her career protecting the waterways and near-shore areas from being over-developed and altered at the Wisconsin Department of National Resources. That is also where she found her current husband, and the love of her life. More than seventeen years ago, she married her former boss and best friend, Ron Fassbender, a gruff, raspy-voiced mountain man.

She acknowledges it took a long time to heal, maybe too long, because she didn't understand that grieving is a necessary step for healing.

Despite all that has happened, she doesn't complain about her life. By 2010, Tere felt strong enough to cowrite her memoir with longtime confidant Logan.

I asked, why fifty years later?

"I felt healed," she said simply. "I knew I was at a good place in my life because of my wonderful husband, my three wonderful children, and my grandchildren ... my life was finally stable."

During a book signing, several of her old teachers came by to show their support, and apologized for not being able to help her all those years earlier. Even relatives told her how sorry they were, for not talking about what happened to her family, and to her.

"They all thought they were doing everything right to protect me, and after my book came out, they just felt horrible that they never talked to me about it—but they were all told not to. My aunt Lois," who she hadn't lived with, "and my cousin said, 'Tere, we're so sorry. We wanted to talk to you so badly.' So it helped a lot of my family too."

That made me wonder once again whether, at least in her case, speaking to the media might have helped her heal sooner. Maybe being out in the open would have encouraged others around her—those relatives, teachers, and friends—to feel comfortable talking to her and helping her through her pain. In fact, Tere spoke fondly about all of the love and support she felt from numerous pen pals she gained, and the countless gifts that were sent to her, because of the intense media coverage that surrounded her tragedy.

Maybe the world's embrace would have helped fill the void left after the death of her parents and siblings; maybe that would have allowed her to grieve for her family.

Of course that was a different era, but after talking to Tere, I believe that there are lessons to be learned from her situation. Perhaps it was being quiet all those years that resulted in her thinking she had conquered the healing process—that she had dealt with her anger and grief and successfully moved on with her life.

Imagine if Tere had come out earlier and purged all of her emotions, working through her pain in the public eye with the media as her conduit; it could have given her a false sense of security, it could have left her feeling used . . . or maybe it would have been just what she needed.

I put the question to Tere: Did she think it would have helped if she would have told her story to the public earlier, rather than waiting fifty years?

She paused, thinking. "I don't know," she said. "It wasn't my decision. I just don't know."

But there was something she knew for sure. "They say you're supposed to grieve. Well, I was supposed to be the brave little girl and so I didn't grieve forever and ever and ever. I didn't realize that was a process you had to go through."

Today, Tere is finally at a good place. She spends her days knitting and walking along Lake Michigan with her husband.

"We're only two blocks away from the lake. We have dogs; I love dogs and other animals. I'm really into our grandchildren and my children. My husband does a lot of hunting and fishing. We do a lot of stuff in the woods. We like a lot of wild game. It's just a very easy life. I read a lot and that's about it; nothing spectacular, but I'm happy as a clam."

WHAT CRIME VICTIMS WANT YOU TO KNOW

Tatsha Robertson

In the past twenty years, I've covered many high-profile tragedies, from the Oklahoma City Bombing to Katrina to September 11, and countless homicides and plane crashes in between. As the former crime editor for the largest magazine in the world, *People* magazine, I sent a platoon of writers, in one year's time, to talk to victims of mass killings in Newtown, Boston, and Aurora.

Journalists covering these crime stories have all had doors slammed in their face. On the other hand, bereaved family members can be decidedly kind and thoughtful to reporters looking to question them at a time when those families are drowning in pain. I can't count the number of times I've heard, "I'm sorry, I just can't talk. I'm so sorry."

But have we journalists shown victims that same kindness? If I had been asked that question a year before this book, I would have said yes. But now, I just don't know.

It may seem like reporters can't wait to chase down grieving family members, but it's an assignment we universally dread. And yet, once we are back in the newsrooms, we pride ourselves on having been sensitive enough to land the "big interview." I, myself, have high-fived reporters returning with "war stories" on how they got their exclusives.

I am not saying that reaction is right or wrong. What I *am* saying is that just because we think we are being sensitive and placing a human face to a tragedy doesn't mean the person we want to interview feels the same way.

As a reporter, I've never once heard a grieving family say, "Ask me anything," as they did with Kim Goldman. Kim is one of them. Joining her on this journey, I've heard things reporters never get to hear, and I've learned things that, as a veteran journalist, you'd think I'd already know. For one, despite the fact that these families allow us in their home at their darkest hours, they are rarely, if ever, comfortable with us—even though we think they are.

I was surprised to hear that families dislike when reporters bring them flowers, a practice common among large publications and television networks. I also learned that while grieving families want to be treated with sensitivity, they don't want *us* crying on *their* shoulders. And they certainly don't want to be treated with kid gloves. Most shocking, everyone we talked to said they want journalists to just tell the truth about what happened to their loved one—*gore* and all. In other words, they don't need us to pretty up their pain. They just want, more than anything else, for the media to get the information right.

These families don't trust us. I'm still wrapping my head around this, but I understand why now, after hearing what they have been through. I feel lucky to have had the chance to experience the other side of the story and, now, to share the lessons I learned with you.

We asked the families featured in this book what advice they would give to the media for speaking with victims. We also asked what advice they would offer other victims as it relates to their interactions with journalists.

Here's what they shared.

Debra Tate

I would like the media to be accurate and honest. The public may not realize this, but before the press comes to us to do any "on the spot news," there's been a whole dialogue behind the scenes and the questions have already been determined, so even if you get a good person that wants to be sensitive and accurate, their bosses, the powers that be, have an agenda, and the reporters have to follow it. My advice: The powers that be need to let things be honest. These are the people that are dictating the public opinion.

Mildred Muhammad

I would tell victims that I'm always alert. I did not feel that being emotional in public was safe. I didn't know how the media would portray that. I was always strategic in how I responded and how much I gave. The media can ask me a question, but that does not mean I have to answer the question in the way they want me to, and I don't have to give it all to them.

Judy Shepard

My advice to victims? You don't owe the media anything. Don't talk to them unless you want to. Don't let them pressure you into doing an interview. Just because they need the story, that's their issue, not yours. Don't do it until you're ready to do it. And here's my advice to the media: Do your homework and tell the truth. Don't state something is a fact unless you know it's a fact. Just because somebody tells a reporter that something is factual doesn't make it so. Do your own research, for crying out loud. Don't reprint somebody else's article.

Marie Monville

We all realize reporters have a job to do, but when they are able to approach the situation based on their heart and based on being a real person, instead of just *this is my job and this is what I want from you*, that is what makes the difference. The reporters that were overly persistent, who didn't seem to have any respect for what I was saying or what I thought was best for my family, left me thinking *I don't want anything to do with them, absolutely nothing.* But on the other hand, the ones who really made an impression on me were the ones who were respectful, and you could tell by the way they approached me that they were thinking with their heart. Those were the ones who I thought about throughout the years—that if I was able to decide on whom to give an interview to, especially when it came to the local reporters, I knew I could trust them.

David Neese

One thing the media should think about is how to be discreet. A lot of times they'll take you out to dinner or lunch, but the reporter needs to talk quietly, so other people can't hear what you're saying. I had one lady sitting there with me in Cracker Barrel and she was just going on and on about everything, and everybody heard her. I'm like, "Maybe we can talk about this another time or something," and I pointed to the people. Reporters need to be sensitive.

Scarlett Lewis

Maybe other victims can learn from my experience with the media: The media was persistent early on but I chose to communicate with them because I wanted to portray my son as he lived, not from what they could piece together from others and assumptions. I was open and honest with them and gave them the details that I wanted others to know about Jesse, so that they could remember those qualities and in turn, honor him. The media I came into contact with were compassionate and reported with care and consideration for how I wanted the story to be portrayed. Moving forward they became helpful as reports were released and questions over details emerged. We would talk and compare notes and I began to understand how important a role they play in truth-finding and even tracking the flow of funds from donations and charities. We built a relationship of trust and to this day I consider some of the local reporters my friends.

Collene Campbell

The media should make darn sure that their reporting is accurate and make sure that they're not reporting untrue facts from a criminal. I think that's the most painful thing—when they listen to a killer and then write and report the untrue facts that that killer says; it hurts the family even more.
And victims? I would hope they would take their unwanted experience and utilize it to help the justice system, to improve the justice system and to help save others.

Kathleen and Scott Larimer

Kathleen: I'd tell other victims of crimes that if you don't want to be out there with the media, close the door. Set perimeters—then they won't take you where you don't want to go.

Scott: My advice to the media is to remember that the loss of somebody through a violent act is a horrible tragedy, but an even bigger tragedy would be to cause harm to the ones who are still alive.

Shirley Wygal

I think that there need to be a few changes [to how media handles reporting on victims]. I think the press needs to have written permission to print my photo. If I call you and say, "Please don't print my photo again," that should be enough. The other thing is, when you're talking to someone who says they are the spokesman for a group of survivors, you might want to ask some other people in the group whether or not that's true. Why not check out the statements made by other people, especially when you are dealing with people who have been victimized? Why would you want to victimize people again?

Esaw and Emerald Garner

Emerald: I would tell other victims that talking about it just helps. Whether it's therapy, talking to somebody at random, or somebody that's close to you, it's good. You can't really give yourself good advice; you're going to be stressed out and you are going to feel like you're at your wits end. You don't know what to do, and you don't know where to turn. For me, going out and listening to other people's stories gave me the confidence to share my story. And as far as media goes? They can be a little bit more respectful about people's space. They don't have to be so close. They could empathize a little more, and not ask you the most insensitive questions.

Esaw: What's my advice to the media? Back up. Give us some time first. You know when a police officer is doing an investigation on a murder and they want to ask you some questions? They always tell you to take a few days to get yourself together. When you feel up to it, come to the precinct and make a report. That's all I would say. Give us some time.

Tere Duperrault Fassbender

My advice to the media is respect the wishes of family and friends as to how much exposure they want. In other words, respect their privacy, because at some point, the survivors and victims will come out and speak, but they will do it on their timeframe. And most importantly, the reporters should get the facts straight. I have to be honest, the media was respectful to my family's wishes. And everything the media wrote about me was basically correct. But I think more recently, reporters jump the gun, they move too quickly and they do not tell the whole story.

FOR MORE INFORMATION

For more information on the families featured in *Media Circus* and their advocacy work:

Debra Tate

Sharon Tate: Recollection, by Debra Tate and Roman Polanski

Tate family website: www.sharontate.net

Mildred Muhammad

Scared Silent: The Mildred Muhammad Story, by Mildred Muhammad

Mildred's personal website: www.mildredmuhammad.com

Judy Shepard

The Meaning of Matthew: My Son's Murder in Laramie, and a World Transformed, by Judy Shepard

Matthew Shepard Foundation: www.matthewshepard.org

Marie Monville

One Light Still Shines: My Life Beyond the Shadow of the Amish Schoolhouse Shooting, by Marie Monville and Cindy Lambert

Marie's personal website: www.mariemonville.com

Dave and Mary Neese

Pretty Little Killers: The Truth Behind the Savage Murder of Skylar Neese by Daleen Berry and Geoffrey C. Fuller

Scarlett Lewis

Nurturing Healing Love: A Mother's Journey of Hope and Forgiveness, by Scarlett Lewis and Natasha Stoynoff

Jesse Lewis Choose Love Foundation: www.jesselewischoose love.org

Collene Campbell

Force 100 and Memory of Victims Everywhere (MOVE): www. force100.org

Scott and Kathleen Larimer

No Notoriety Campaign: www.nonotoriety.com

Esaw and Emerald Garner

National Action Network: www.nationalactionnetwork.net

Tere Dupperault Fassbender

Alone: Orphaned on the Ocean, by Tere Duperrault Fassbender and Richard Logan

ADDITIONAL REFERENCES

Can't Forgive: My 20-Year Battle with O. J. Simpson, by Kim Goldman

Manson: The Life and Times of Charles Manson, by Jeff Guinn

Newtown: An American Tragedy, by Matthew Lysiak

Mickey Thompson: The Fast Life and Tragic Death of a Racing Legend, by Eric Arneson

ACKNOWLEDGMENTS

From Kim:

I have the good fortune to be surrounded by so many incredible people who are always in my corner—and I am deeply appreciative for their love, support, and encouragement. As much as I want to list every single one of you, I am just highlighting a select few that continue to have a profound influence in my life.

To my dearest friends and biggest cheerleaders, Denise, Erika, Jackie, Lisa, Michele, Reneé—ladies, I love you all so much. You always give me a much-needed reality check or laugh just at the right time—I am one lucky broad.

To my two most favorite boys, my dad and my son. Dad, thank you for always believing in me and being my biggest fan; I'd be lost without you! Sam, thanks for your patience with my long hours spent talking and writing—I loved hearing you say, "It's okay, Mom, I am proud of you." You both are my inspiration. I love you with all of my heart.

To Leslie Garson and Michael Wright, for partnering with me on my writing adventures. It's been amazing to share this journey with you both. Mike, thanks for being such a good sounding board and for always having my best interests in mind. And Leslie, thank you for your brutal honesty—it is always spot on. Love you both!

To Tatsha—what a whirlwind this has been! Thank you for believing in this project and trusting in the process. Thank you for your wisdom, guidance, honesty, and humor. I've learned so much from you in such a short time. I will miss the "coffee house"!

To all of the families that allowed me into their homes and their hearts in preparation for this book—thank you for trusting me. Your raw emotion and honesty far exceeded my expectations and will leave a lasting impression, deeper than you can ever imagine.

From Tatsha:

First and foremost, many thanks to Jacquie Flynn for introducing me to the world of book publishing and smooches to KC Baker for believing in me.

Hugs to Destiny "Quick Fingers" Perez, who did yeoman's work as our transcriber. A collective high five to my Saturday writing workshop buddies for cheering me on, especially my friend Roslyn Karpel. And a big thanks to the workshop's leader, Jeff Ourvan, who graciously agreed to read various drafts. A giant squeeze to my best girlfriends, otherwise known as "my board of directors": Rosalind Bentley; Kristal Brent Zook; Carol Kelly; Kemba Dunham; Kyla Upshaw Croal, one of my sisters; Vanessa Karen Du Luca; and to the late Jonell Nash, for your support.

Much love to the Goldman family, especially Kim Goldman, whose big, lovely heart has taught me more about storytelling than any journalism school ever did.

And last but not least, thank you to my huge, supportive family, especially my mother, Marcia Robertson, and my dear husband, Nico, for his love and undying support.

From Kim and Tatsha:

We are more than grateful to everyone at BenBella, especially Glenn Yeffeth and our brilliant editor Leah Wilson, whose insightful direction helped guide us on this journey. A heartfelt thanks to other BenBella family members, including Sarah

Dombrowsky, Monica Lowry, Adrienne Lang, Alicia Kania, and Jennifer Canzoneri.

To the media, we know your job is difficult. We haven't forgotten that you cover hundreds of horrific crimes every year and that can't be easy, seeing such darkness in the world—we know that takes a toll. This book, we hope, will help make it a little easier for the next time you encounter a victim's family.

ABOUT THE AUTHORS

Known nationwide as a victims' rights advocate after her brother's murder and the infamous O. J. Simpson murder trial, **Kim Goldman** is the founding Co-Chair of The Ron Goldman Foundation for Justice. She is also the Executive Director of The Youth Project, a non-profit organization that provides free counseling, support groups, crisis intervention, and education and outreach to thousands of teenagers since opening in 2000. In her spare time, Goldman travels the country as an impassioned public speaker on victims' rights, the role of the media, judicial reform, and other related topics. She is currently a resident of Greater Los Angeles, where she has lived for thirteen years, and a single parent. See more online at KimberlyGoldman.com.

Former magazine editor **Tatsha Robertson** is an award-winning editor and writer with more than twenty years of experience handling investigative, feature, and news stories for leading magazines and newspapers. As the first female NYC Bureau Chief and National Rover for *The Boston Globe*, she covered some of the nation's largest stories, including Katrina, September 11th, and many major crime stories. She pioneered *Essence* magazine's focus on investigative and news articles, which led to the positioning of the magazine as a significant authority and voice on news and led to an interview with President Obama. Most recently, she was the crime editor at *People Magazine*. Robertson is a frequent guest on national media, appearing on programs like *The Today Show*, CNN, HLN, FOX, and MSNBC. Tatsha teaches journalism as an adjunct professor at NYU. She is currently partnered with Harvard University's Achievement Gap Initiative in coauthoring a book on academic achievement.